CRITICAL ACCLAIM
FOR GUTSY WOMEN

"The book is essential reading for women travelers of any age."
—*Chicago Tribune*

"The perfect bon voyage gift for your favorite woman traveler."
—*Living Fit Magazine*

"A nuts-and-bolts approach to women's travel . . . seasoned advice geared both to novices and veterans."
—*USA Today*

"Packed with instructive and inspiring travel vignettes and tips . . . it is not just for adventure seekers or solo travelers."
—*Boston Globe*

"How do you cope with an impulse to take wing? How do you handle desires to find adventures in exotic cultures . . . ? If you're Marybeth Bond, you promptly leap aboard such urges, ride them where they happen to take you, then seek to lead others by word and example."
—*San Francisco Chronicle*

"If you've got the bug to get out but are leery of the less-beaten path, check out *Gutsy Women*. Bond has packed this paperback with handy advice."
—*Women's Sports & Fitness*

"Fresh and insightful, even for the most-seasoned traveler."
—*Washington Post*

"Gutsy Women is a wonderful gift for a woman traveling . . . and features engaging stories and personal advice by women travelers . . ."
—*Chicago Herald*

GUTSY WOMEN

Advice, Inspiration, Stories

GUTSY WOMEN

Advice, Inspiration, Stories

Fourth Edition

MARYBETH BOND

Travelers' Tales
Palo Alto

Travelers' Tales and Solas House are trademarks of Solas House, Inc., 853 Alma Street, Palo Alto, California 94301. www.travelerstales.com

Cover design: Stefan Gutermuth
Cover illustration: Melissa Sweet
Interior design: Scribe Inc.
Page layout: Scribe Inc., using the fonts Dante, Gill Sans, Marker Felt, and Wade Sans
Production: Natalie Baszile

Library of Congress Cataloging-in-Publication Data
Bond, Marybeth.
  Gutsy women: more travel tips and wisdom for the road / Marybeth Bond.
  —4th ed.
    p. cm.
  ISBN 978-160952-064-9 (pbk.)
  1. Travel. 2. Women travelers. I. Title.

G151.B66 2007
910.2'02—dc22   2007016420

Fourth Edition
Printed in the United States
10 9 8 7 6 5 4 3 2 1

For my family
for encouraging me to fulfill my passion to travel—
with and without them.

TABLE OF CONTENTS

INTRODUCTION

———

WHAT'S A GUTSY WOMAN? To me, gutsy means courageous and women today are courageous in a twenty-first century way. We buy our own cars and homes, and we are open to adventure—whether it's climbing Mount Everest, biking across the USA, or running for a "cause." Gutsy women are bold, strong and savvy, not foolish and naïve. The tips and wisdom that fill the pages of this edition of *Gutsy Women* will empower, energize, and inspire you. Even if you're not sure if you are a Gutsy Woman, this book will allow you to discover her within you.

In terms of travel, our habits have changed too. After all, women make 80 percent of the travel decisions, and we're on the go. We are getting off the beaten track and trekking the globe, on our own and with other women.

If your partner isn't interested in traveling, or not to the places you may want to visit, then I encourage you to find friends who are. If a friend is too busy or your schedules don't synch, book yourself on an all-women's tour and you'll probably meet some travel companions for your next adventure. Your first trip without the company of a close friend or spouse doesn't have to be to the other side of the world. It can be a journey close to home—somewhere you've always wanted to go—somewhere just to get your feet wet. Even if you are already a seasoned traveler, I'm sure you will learn something new and useful in this expanded edition of *Gutsy Women*.

Over the past thirty years I have hiked, cycled, climbed, dived, and kayaked my way through more than ninety countries, from the depths of the Flores Sea to the summit of Mount Kilimanjaro. I traveled alone around the world for two years at the age of twenty-nine, wandered the globe with my husband (who I met in Kathmandu when I was thirty), and more recently I have explored this bountiful and beautiful earth with my daughters and girlfriends.

In the process of creating twelve travel books, including nine for Travelers' Tales and three for National Geographic, I have discovered what women want in their travel experiences: safety, freedom, adventure, opportunities for learning and giving back, and time to nurture ourselves. I have interviewed hundreds of gutsy women who have shared their stories, their wisdom, and their strength with me and through this book with you, too.

We discover the world as we physically move around the planet; we discover ourselves on the inner journey that accompanies our travels. The rewards are many: We try on new identities as more independent, self-sufficient women; we explore new behaviors; and we develop a greater awareness of our potential.

So be a gutsy woman and go forth to change yourself and the world. See you on the road!

THE FIRST STEP

We generate fears while we sit; we overcome them by action.
Fear is nature's warning signal to get busy.
—*Pacific Crest Outward Bound School, Book of Readings*

———

PREPARING YOURSELF MENTALLY AND emotionally for traveling overseas is just as important as getting your visas and shots. Give yourself time to work through fears you may have about safety, traveling alone or in a group of unknown companions, or fitting into a different culture. To convert your apprehension into excitement, begin your mental preparation weeks or even months prior to departure. Get in touch with women who have gone before you. Connect with them by phone, e-mail, or by reading their stories in travel books or blogs.

It is reassuring before you take your trip to have an itinerary, guidebooks, research from the Internet. One of the most valuable sources of up-to-date information are other travelers you'll meet along the way, locals you will encounter on trains or at bus stops, or the staff at tourist offices, hotels, and bed-and-breakfasts. Fight the urge to organize everything before you go. Spontaneity and flexibility are the creative forces behind meaningful journeys. Try to avoid overscheduling and overplanning.

At age twenty-nine, when I left on my around-the-world journey, I had a detailed itinerary that I

> The trick is not to rid your stomach of butterflies, but to make them fly in formation.
>
> ♦
>
> —*Pacific Crest Outward Bound School, Book of Readings*

3

abandoned on day three in Bangkok. If I had followed my original plans, I never would have met Danielle, a Swiss nurse with whom I traveled for a month, stayed with a Muslim family on a houseboat in Kashmir, or hiked for a week with another new travel friend among the ethnic tribes of northern Thailand. It is tempting to follow a structured itinerary on long or short trips. Recently, on a weeklong trip to Paris, I lost all the notes a friend gave me with restaurant and shopping recommendations. Instead of reliving her trip, I discovered my own, more relaxed version of the City of Light. I dined *en plein air* at a sidewalk restaurant on the seventeenth-century Place des Vosges and visited three museums in one day, instead of searching for my friend's favorite shops.

I never regretted any trip I took, no matter how inconvenient or expensive it seemed at the planning stage. I only regret the trips I didn't take.

TIPS

> Buy your airline tickets on Tuesday or Wednesday. Although it is not always the case, here's the typical scenario: An airline announces a fare sale on Monday, and on Tuesday other airlines match the price or undercut it. On Wednesday, the fare war is in high gear. By Thursday most of the cheap fares are gone. Saturday is the worst day to buy a ticket. Airlines usually raise their prices late on Friday night to see if other airlines will, too. If no one follows suit, then fares may go back down by Monday.

> Learn a few words in the local language—hello, good-bye, please, thank you, beautiful. If you have the time, take a language course.

> Seek out people who have traveled or lived in the country you'll be visiting and ask them lots of questions, especially about good reading material and whether they know citizens from there now living in the U.S.

> Go online and browse through the travel chat rooms or do a hashtag search on Twitter. You may make contact with

interesting people from the country where you plan to travel. Often when you arrive you'll have a name and phone number of someone to look up.

If you join Servas (www.servas.org) you'll stay in private homes with locals who want to host you. See the Resources section for more details.

♦

—MB

➤ Consider staying at a family-run guesthouse, bed-and-breakfast or couch surf. Local families in many countries treat their guests like long-lost relatives. They'll cook local specialties, play their music, and share their evenings with you.

➤ Eat out at a local restaurant that serves authentic food from the country you plan to visit.

➤ Reduce your anxiety when visiting a new country— prearrange transportation from the airport to your accommodations, especially if you arrive at night. It's so reassuring to be met by a professional driver at the airport displaying a sign with your name on it. I often book a transfer for arrivals in Africa and India. The driver helps me get my luggage and work my way safely through the throng of touts, beggars, and men offering their services as porters.

➤ Fuel your passion by planning your trip around a special interest such as art, cooking, biking, gardening, etc. If you love gardening, do targeted online research to find famous gardens you can visit at your destination, whether it is in England, India, or Japan. Contact the local tourist bureau and ask if there are historic house tours, kitchen tours, or garden tours you can take. Consider taking a cooking class in Italy, France, or Thailand. Local organizations may be able to provide helpful information about these activities at your destination. You will meet other like-minded individuals if you pursue your interests while traveling.

- Consider doing some volunteer work as part of your travels. Getting involved in volunteer organizations offers a great opportunity to deepen your experience and helps you get beneath the surface of a culture. See Chapter 20 for more information.

- To avoid feeling overwhelmed by your impending departure, allow enough time to prepare, logistically and mentally.

- You will greatly reduce the stress associated with your departure if you begin packing several days in advance. You will then have time to replace a missing button or wash favorite clothes before taking off.

- Checklists can be handy for keeping track of packing, good-byes to friends, closing up the house, putting a "vacation response" on your email and other necessary tasks.

- Take along personal photos of your friends, family, and pets.

- Prebook your first night's accommodation. Chances are you'll feel more comfortable in a new environment if you have a plan—where you're going (hotel, guest house, youth hostel) and how you'll get there (taxi, public transportation, rental car).

- Contact the establishment of your first night's stay, ask if they offer a shuttle from the airport. If not, what should a taxi cost? Is there a convenient, safe local bus or subway? Can they recommend a local car rental agency? (They are often less expensive than national chains.) Find answers to these questions and you'll arrive more confident and know how to proceed.

- Pack lightly. If you cannot carry your bag from your bedroom to the car when you are leaving, you know you will have trouble carrying it from the taxi to the lobby of your hotel or from the train platform to your train compartment. Most travelers worry about handling their luggage, so rethink what you've packed and lighten up!

- Traveler's insurance can cover a wide range of mishaps and emergencies, from trip cancellation, trip interruption, baggage and trip delay, and lost or stolen baggage, to rental car collision damage waiver, rental car personal accident insurance, accident medical expenses, and in-hospital indemnity. Call your insurance company to verify what their policy covers, particularly medical coverage overseas. If you will be traveling on a shoestring, independently, or to developing countries, medical evacuation insurance is essential. Verify that your evacuation insurance covers you not just to the nearest hospital, but all the way home.

➤ To make the day of your departure easier, give yourself plenty of time to get to the airport, train, or bus station. Be packed and ready to go the night before.

➤ Be easy on yourself when you get back from a trip.

II
SAFETY AND SECURITY

Use your city smarts. Try to avoid potentially dicey places like a
deserted street in a big city. If you are alone, don't walk down it.
Having other people around is your best safety insurance.

—*Susan Spano, Los Angeles Times*

———

THE MOMENT WE STEP out the door, we are aware of the foot-
steps behind us. We are concerned for our personal safety and with
good reason. Safety and security are primary concerns for women,
especially those traveling to unfamiliar places. To travel without fear,
we need to arm ourselves with common sense and a flexible attitude.

We can avoid questionable neighborhoods. We can communicate that we are self-assured by walking confidently with our heads
up. We can be aware of our surroundings. If we apply the common
sense we use at home, we can feel safe virtually anywhere.

One thing is certain: The more you travel the less fear you will
experience.

When in doubt, ask a lot of questions or ask for help.

GENERAL SAFETY TIPS

- ➢ Use the common sense you've learned over the years. If you
  wouldn't walk in an unknown neighborhood after dark at
  home, do not do it overseas.

- ➢ In Third World countries, carry your valuables, including
  train tickets, money, passports, in a money belt or pouch.
  Keep only what you need for the day in your purse or
  daypack.

- ➤ Whether traveling by bus, train, plane, or boat, try to sit next to another woman if you want to avoid potential come-ons. You may well make a new friend.

- ➤ If you plan on staying in hostels, take a combination lock with you to secure your backpack to your bed or in a locker if you are leaving your room. It is also useful to attach your backpack to the luggage rack in a train compartment.

> Trust your instincts. Let me repeat that: Trust your instincts. Instincts are not a matter of consensus. If you feel something is off, wrong, strange—get out, move on, flee, whatever is appropriate. Do it quickly.
>
> ◆
>
> —MB

- ➤ It can be very difficult to know what is considered offensive or suggestive in segregated societies, such as orthodox Muslim areas. At times you may feel uncomfortable or vulnerable. You may not know if the local men view you as a sex symbol or immoral. So take your cues from the local women. Blend in. Dress appropriately. Ask other Western women who have experience in this culture for their advice.

- ➤ Use your judgment at public demonstrations or political rallies with massive crowds. Sometimes they can become violent and should be avoided, while other times attending such gatherings can be enlightening. If you have doubts, stay near the edge of the crowd.

> To ward off unwanted male attention, especially in male-dominated countries, consider wearing a fake wedding ring if you are traveling alone.
>
> ◆
>
> —MB

- ➤ When traveling by train or bus, look for other women or families to sit with. If you are seated with someone, it is unlikely that you will be approached or harassed. Ask for help or company if you feel uncomfortable.

Alarming reports confirm an increase in date rape drugging. Increasingly young women in foreign countries and the U.S. have a drink with a stranger and wake up the next morning, nude, raped, and robbed. They have no recollection of what happened. Rohypnol, "the date rape drug," is odorless, tasteless, and colorless. It is a tranquilizer that can be easily slipped into your drink. Do not accept a drink that you didn't see poured. Do not leave your glass unattended.

♦

—MB

> If a group of men or young boys approaches you on the sidewalk, cross to the other side of the street to give them space and you peace of mind.

> If you are being followed on the street and you feel threatened, duck into a shop and firmly tell the clerk: "I am a foreigner and someone is following me. I am frightened and need help." If need be, have the clerk call a taxi or the police for you.

> Scam artists such as thieves and pickpockets create distractions as a cover-up. Beware of people who accidentally spill something on your clothing, bump into you, or drop a piece of luggage in front of you. This is the time to watch your luggage and keep a hand on your valuables. Don't underestimate the skill of rip-off artists—they can misdirect your attention no matter how watchful you are.

> Study a map before you leave your lodging or car so that once on the street you know where you are

Always carry enough money in your shoe to get you out of a tight spot. Be willing to spend this money on a cab in order to get you to a safe place or back to your lodging. Do not take unnecessary risks.

♦

—MB

headed. Try to avoid struggling with a map or looking like a tourist.

➤ Stay alert when getting off a bus or train or riding an escalator, as this is when pickpockets tend to strike.

➤ When asking for directions, approach women with children or families.

➤ In the winter, the sun sets quickly. A bustling market can quickly empty out and be transformed into dark, deserted streets. Plan ahead. Return to a safe, busy neighborhood by dark.

➤ Put a note in your passport with instructions explaining who to call, your blood type, any serious allergies to medicines.

➤ Be aware of your surroundings (people, cars, doorways, stairwells) and have a plan in case you get into a dangerous situation. Be prepared to act quickly, scream for help, kick, and run.

➤ Never volunteer that you are traveling alone.

➤ Know where you're going before setting out in a rental car.

➤ Do not reveal a map in your car.

➤ Write your first initial and last name on your luggage tags to conceal your gender. Or use laminated business cards as luggage tags so that strangers do not know your home address.

Dress conservatively. Clothing that is fashionable and appropriate at home may project a provocative image in another culture. Leave the revealing clothing at home.

◆

—*MB*

Serendipity is at the heart of all travel. Once you are on the road, if you take small risks such as talking to a local person or accepting an invitation to someone's home, often your reward will be experiences you will long remember.

◆

—*MB*

- When alone (particularly at night), walk with the crowd and act as if you're part of the pack.

- If you will be arriving after dark, rental car companies and hotels can arrange for someone to accompany you to and from parking lots.

- If you are traveling alone, choose national hotel chains with interior room entrances, as opposed to motel-style outside entrances. More and more women are also choosing small inns and bed-and-breakfasts where the proprietors are more aware of their activities and will become alarmed if they don't return by a specific time.

- In some developing countries you may be hassled by men in airport terminals who offer cheap transportation into town. Don't accept their offers. Seek out a ground transportation desk near the baggage claim area for assistance.

ROAD TRIP SAFETY TIPS

- Plan your driving time during daylight hours and lock your doors when you get into your vehicle.

- When entering your car, look into the back to make sure no one is hiding inside.

- If you are parked next to a van be cautious and enter your car from the door opposite where the van is parked. Many serial killers attack their victims by pulling them into their vans.

- As soon as you enter your automobile, lock the doors. Do not sit in a parking lot and eat, work, or sleep. This makes you a target.

- Restrooms at truck stops, gas stations, and public rest stops can be unsafe. Stop at moderate hotels that are likely to have a lobby, as they will usually have a clean and safe public restroom and other amenities like phones, soft drink machines, and newspaper dispensers.

➤ Crime in hotel and airport parking lots is increasing. Pay attention to where you park—look for parking spaces under lights, close to the hotel entrance or terminal. Often the "off-airport" lots are safer. The shuttle bus picks you up at your car, takes you to the terminal, and drops you off at your car again. If it is dark and you feel uncomfortable, ask the driver to wait until you are safely inside your car.

➤ When you rent a car, ask for an up-to-date map and directions to your first meeting or hotel. If you are in a city you don't know, ask which neighborhoods can be dangerous. With the help of the rental car representative, cross off the dangerous areas on your map, so you don't accidentally drive through or stop in an unsafe area.

➤ If someone yells or honks at you, indicates that there is something wrong, or bumps your car while you are driving, do not stop. Drive to a well-lit, busy place and then check it out. Don't stop where there aren't people nearby.

➤ Be sure your spare tire is inflated and that you know how to change it. For added security, always carry a can of "Fix a Flat" spray in the trunk and become a member of AAA.

➤ Carry your cell phone. Keep it close at hand, not in your purse or in the back seat. Program 911 into the automatic dial feature.

HOTEL SAFETY

➤ When you check in, register using your last name and your first initial only. Also ask that your room number not be announced. If they say your room number aloud, ask to be put in another room

➤ At check-in, request a room on the second to the sixth floors. Thieves target rooms on the ground level with easy escape access, and some fire hoses cannot reach above the sixth floor.

- Hang out the "Do Not Disturb" sign and leave the TV on when you leave your room. This will discourage anyone from entering your room while you are away.

- Place your room key in the same location. I always put it on top of the TV. In the event of an emergency, you will want to have time to take the key with you, allowing for your quick return if it was only a fire drill. You don't want to be caught in the hallway in a skimpy nightgown and then have to wait at the front desk for another key to be issued. Leave it on the television or on the bedside table.

- Pack a rubber doorstop. This provides added security in your hotel room. Use it either on the main door or an adjoining room door that may not have double locks.

- Secure all of the locks on hotel room doors whenever you are in the room. You could be in the bathroom and not hear someone knock. You don't want anyone to enter the room while you are inside, even to check the mini-bar or turn down your sheets.

- Play it safe and avoid displaying your hotel room key in public. Don't leave it on your restaurant table or on the chair by the swimming pool—it could be stolen or someone could read the name of your hotel and your room number.

- If someone knocks on your hotel room door, verify who it is. If there is a peephole, use it. If the person identifies him- or herself as a hotel employee, request that they come back later, when you've left the room. If they insist on entering, call the front desk and confirm that someone from the staff needs to enter your room and for what purpose before letting anyone in.

- If you fill out the room service breakfast order form that you hang on your door after hours, do not divulge your first name (which indicates you are female) or the number of people eating. This advertises that you are a woman and alone for the night.

- Request a room near the elevators and away from any renovation work. Have your key out when you leave the elevator.

- Lock valuables in a safe at the front desk or in your room—even while you are in the shower.

- If your bag is stolen from the hotel, report it immediately and recruit management to search for it. Most hotel robberies are committed by staff members. Many hotels do not let their staff leave with packages, so the thieves often take the money and dump the rest on the premises.

III
Keeping in Touch

I send my words into the world and wait for
whatever new words will come.
—*Georgia Heard, Writing Toward Home*

———

DEPENDING UPON WHERE YOU are going and how long you
are staying, keeping in touch with home may be as simple as making a phone call or sending an e-mail or text message. If you are
planning a trip of a month or longer—especially in developing
countries and remote areas—you'll need to prepare yourself to
live comfortably without correspondence from home for periods
of time.

Create your own travel blog so your friends and family can read
about your trip as it happens. Post photos and use Facebook, Twit-
ter, Google+ for interacting with those at home, and people you
meet on the road. Best of all, you can't lose it, get it dirty, or spill
beer on it.

Today, internet connections are available all over the world, from
ice cream shops in San Miguel, Mexico, to local bars in small French
villages. Internet access is even available in remote locations like
northern Thailand or the island of Tonga. Getting online is becoming less expensive and more accessible worldwide. So do not hesitate to stay in touch with your loved ones by e-mail or Skype. It is
also handy if you need to download maps or do more research on
the town you are in.

TIPS

➤ Be sure to pack a copy of your address book. Do not take your original. Make a copy and paste it into an email to yourself.

➤ E-mail is often the best way to stay in touch. Check with other travelers or the desk clerk at your lodging to find the closest cybercafé or free wireless hot spot.

➤ Many people still prefer communicating home by telephone. There are so many telephone company and card options now that even a simple long-distance call can be complicated. Know how to use your phone card to make long-distance calls before you leave on a trip and keep the access number for your long distance carrier in an easy-to-locate place in your address book.

➤ You can sign up for an International Plan, but they are complex and confusing. You may have to pay for all incoming calls, even those you don't answer but go into your voice mail. Ask lots of questions so you can understand the terms.

➤ Everyone wonders if their cell phone will work in Europe. The best way to find out for sure is to check with your cell phone provider. For example, on the AT&T Wireless Web site you can type in the names of the countries you plan to visit and your phone model and then find the price for voice and data services on your phone.

➤ Before you pick up your cell phone and make lots of calls from abroad, study the price list per country and per minute. You may be shocked by the high cost of International roaming. Calls from overseas back to the USA can hit $4.50 per minute and higher.

➤ Don't even think about using your domestic cell phone's plan for data retrieval overseas: Downloading an attachment or Web information can easily cost you $10 a page.

➤ There is a cheaper and more cost-effective way: Buy a cheap cell phone overseas with the foreign SIM card in it. They don't usually cost more than $40. In Asia they're much less expensive than in Europe.

➢ In numerous countries, including Ireland, France, Chile, Mexico and Thailand, I bought a pre-paid calling card. They are available at Tabac stands in France and in small convenience stores in other countries. Confirm with the vendor that the card is for International calls. Then you can make calls from your hotel room or any phone. It's simple. You call a toll-free 800 number and use the pin number. Before you make every call you'll be told how many minutes remain on the card.

➢ Give a detailed itinerary to loved ones before you leave and include your email addresses. Then ask your family or friends to email you once or twice during your trip.

➢ If your journey is going to be unstructured and spontaneous, send e-mails to keep people up to date as your plans develop, should there be an emergency at home.

➢ Stay in touch with yourself, keep a journal.

IV

HEALTH AND HYGIENE ON THE ROAD

*The rewards of the journey far outweigh the
risk of leaving the harbor.*

—Unknown

WHEN I RETURN FROM an exotic place, the first thing many people ask me is, "Did you get sick?" They want to know, specifically, if I got traveler's diarrhea. Yes, that is my most common travel-related illness. To avoid it, I am careful about what I eat and drink. Eating dairy products is a hit-or-miss affair. You wouldn't want to pass up creamy pastries in Paris or gelato in Italy, but you will need to think twice before eating the same products in a developing country where refrigeration, sanitation, and pasteurization is spotty.

If you plan to travel out of the country, see your dentist prior to your trip for a complete check up. Have him or her look for loose fillings or unstable caps.

Buy temporary filling material and toothache medication at the drug store. And always have one or two strong pain relief pills in your cosmetic kit. Be sure to leave them in the original prescription bottle, so customs won't ask you questions about unidentified pills.

—MB

What about eating at food stalls? You have to take a few chances to have some wonderful culinary encounters and, yes, even risk getting sick. In Southeast Asia, some of the best food available is found in the street stalls. You'll have to do some investigating, though. Ask other travelers and locals where it is safe to eat. Look for crowded places.

Preparation and precaution will help you stay healthy.

TIPS

➤ Wash your hands often and always carry antibacterial gel while you travel.

➤ In countries with questionable sanitation, avoid the tap water. Don't brush your teeth with tap water, rinse your mouth in the shower, or put ice cubes in your drinks. Drink only bottled or treated water. When you buy bottled water be sure to see it opened in your presence. Eat only salads and fruit that you have prepared and peeled yourself.

>
> On a monthlong trek in the Himalayas, the most appreciated gift I shared with fellow trekkers was the use of my sunscreen and chapstick. My lips seem to dry out and crack from the moment I step on the plane.
>
> ◆
>
> —MB

➤ I swear by Pepto Bismol and Alka Seltzer tablets. I recommend you pack an ample supply.

➤ If you get diarrhea, consume fluids, eat bland, dry foods, and rest. Consider short-term use of Imodium or Ciprofloxacin. I always travel with Ciprofloxacin, which is an all-purpose antibiotic that can be used for upper respiratory problems or serious traveler's diarrhea. You'll need a prescription for it, so plan ahead. If your symptoms don't go away after self-treatment, see a doctor.

➤ Antinausea pills, such as dimenhydrinate (brand name Dramamine), are the most common over-the-counter medications used by travelers. However, side effects include drowsiness and dry mouth. For it to be effective, you must start taking it a day before your departure. If you are going on a long trip, you may want to get a prescription from your doctor for scopolamine—a thumbnail-size skin patch that you wear behind your ear.

➤ Pressure point bracelets help many queasy travelers. Put them on your wrists several hours before you take off. Another form of relief is taking capsules of powdered ginger (940 mg)—available at health food stores—before a trip. I also pack candied ginger and ginger snap cookies to munch en route.

Beat Blisters! Long walks on trails or on uneven surfaces like cobblestone streets can cause blisters. Band-aids often slip off toes and heels. Pack thin moleskin in your purse or backpack. Leave new shoes at home. Old shoes that are broken-in are the most comfortable.

♦

—*MB*

➤ For information on inoculations and all health concerns, log on to the National Centers for Disease Control and Prevention (CDC) Web site, www.cdc.gov/travel. They also have a toll-free number, 800-CDC-INFO (800-232-4636). The CDC will give you access to important health-related travel information, including links on vaccinations and food-and-water-borne illnesses.

➤ You may have the worst menstrual period of your life so don't forget a pain reliever for cramps. Pack a generous supply of tampons and panty liners.

➤ When traveling for extended periods of time and crossing multiple time zones, many women experience a temporary cessation of their periods. This can cause confusion about when to take birth control pills or if a pregnancy has begun.

➤ In hot, humid climates, yeast infections are a common travel ailment. Taking antibiotics and wearing a wet bathing suit or tight pants, shorts, or panty hose can contribute to the infection. To avoid yeast infections, wear loose clothing that allows air to circulate. Cotton is better than silk or nylon. If you are prone to yeast infections, don't leave home without your medication.

➤ Skirts with elastic waists are comfortable in all types of weather. In heat, they allow air to circulate up your legs and thus reduce the incidence of yeast infections. They are also convenient when you need to use a squat toilet or when you have to go in the bushes.

➤ Be wary of swimming in tropical fresh water. Stagnant water can be home to snails carrying the tiny larvae that cause schistosomiasis, a dangerous disease that can damage body organs. The larvae will cause your skin to itch. Drying yourself vigorously with a towel immediately after exposure may remove most of the larvae. Before wading in, ask locals about the likelihood of such snails in the water.

➤ In developing countries it may be tempting to get an inexpensive manicure, have your ears pierced, take an acupuncture treatment, or even get a tattoo, but be careful with any activities that might puncture your skin.

➤ Cold water, ice, cold cream, or toothpaste will reduce severe itching. If in the wilderness, try using mud. If you are prone to poison oak or poison ivy, wear long pants and be prepared with special poison ivy soap.

➤ Prevent ticks and mosquito bites by using bug spray. Spray your pants, socks, and around your ankles, neck, and back.

➤ What should be in your medical kit? See the packing list in the Resources section at the end of this book.

➤ Active travelers should pack moleskin for blisters, extra socks, comfortable shoes, sunscreen, sun hats, visors, and Vaseline to apply between toes, under bra straps, and anywhere else you might experience friction.

➤ Pack total sunblock or a very high SPF sunscreen. It can be expensive, difficult or impossible to find high-protection sunscreens overseas. Sun, wind, water, and snow reflection can damage multiple layers of skin.

> If you exercise regularly at home, consider jogging in the morning on your trip. Ask hotel personnel or a local person about safety and a suggestion for a scenic route. Dress modestly in loose-fitting clothes.

> Avoid going barefoot, especially in hostel showers. This will prevent fungal and parasitic infections as well as minimize the chance of foot cuts and injuries. Try to keep your feet clean and dry.

I always pack my running shoes, and whenever I run, I'm rewarded with a sightseeing gem. I've jogged on mountain trails in Japan, around Tiananmen Square in Beijing, through a forest in Holland, and across San Francisco's Golden Gate Bridge. I always run in the morning to catch a glimpse of how locals greet the day.

♦

—*Alison Ashton, San Diego, California*

> Although we all love animals, overseas, avoid petting them. Even if dogs or cats seem clean and friendly, a bite from an animal while traveling could lead to a serious disease such as rabies.

> Pack strong pain relief pills. Be sure to leave them in the original bottle, so customs won't ask you questions about unidentified pills. If you dislocate a shoulder or have a tooth ache, you'll be happy to self-medicate until you get to a hospital.

> Drink plenty of bottled water to keep yourself hydrated and healthy.

> Avoid all but emergency gynecological examinations and treatment in developing countries. Inadequately sterilized instruments can spread sexually transmitted diseases.

> Do not take chances if having sex—always use latex condoms to reduce the risk of HIV and other sexually transmitted diseases.

> Women can safely scuba dive during menstruation. Don't believe the stories of menstrual blood attracting sharks. Most

women use tampons, which reduce blood loss to almost nothing.

➤ The U.S. National Park Service issues leaflets that advise women not to hike in bear country during their menstrual periods. Bears do pick up human scents, but no research has proven that black or grizzly bears are specifically attracted by menstruation odors.

➤ If you are taking oral contraceptives, you may encounter problems if you contract traveler's diarrhea or an upset stomach. Your birth control pills may not be absorbed from your intestinal tract and you may be without protection. Doctors recommend that if you vomit within three hours of taking a pill, take another one. After severe intestinal problems your birth control pills may not be effective. Always carry a backup method of contraception if you plan to be sexually active. Condoms are often unavailable or of poor quality in the developing world.

➤ Motor vehicle crashes are a leading cause of injury among travelers, so walk and drive defensively. Avoid travel at night, if possible, and use seatbelts when they are available.

➤ If you do get sick and need to seek professional medical services, try to find hospitals that serve the international community in major cities overseas. Call your embassy or ask the concierge at a good hotel for a reference.

Fight microbes by washing your hands in the morning, before eating, and after visiting the bathroom. In public toilets, many people have touched everywhere you will touch, including the door handle, so use your hand sanitizer after you exit the restroom and don't rub your nose or eyes.

◆

—MB

HOW TO DEAL WITH JET LAG

➤ Staying warm while you fly relaxes you. The temperature on airplanes can vary from tropical heat to arctic chill, and you cannot always count on having a blanket provided by the airline. Dress in layers and bring a sweater. Take everything you'll need out of your carry-on bag before you stash it overhead or under the seat in front of you.

➤ Wear loose-fitting clothes. Frequent international travelers choose comfortable slacks or long skirts so they can easily cross their legs. Avoid tight socks or nylon knee-high stockings. If they leave a mark on your leg, then they're too tight.

➤ If you can, place your feet on top of your carry-on bags that are stowed beneath the seat in front of you. Keep them raised off the floor to increase circulation and minimize swelling.

➤ Be conscious of your posture in the plane seat. Use the pillow offered by the airline to support your lower back. Do in-seat exercises, walk around the plane, and stretch as much as possible. Be aware of posture and movement as you get up, lift or retrieve your carry-on bag from the overhead compartment and deplane. This is when back injuries can occur.

➤ A travel pillow for your neck is a good investment. They are inexpensive and readily available; most international airports have luggage and accessory stores that carry them. A travel pillow keeps the head up and prevents pulled muscles.

➤ Avoid drinks or snacks high in sodium such as Bloody or Virgin Marys, pretzels, and peanuts. Read the labels. If you consume too much salt during a long trip, your feet may swell so much you won't be able to put your shoes back on. I've seen people walk off the plane in socks, carrying their shoes.

➤ Drink a lot of water and avoid alcohol and caffeine. Eight ounces of water per hour is recommended. Not only will this keep you hydrated, it will force you to get up and use the bathroom, thus getting you up and stretching your muscles.

➢ Carry your own water bottle aboard and ask the flight attendant to fill it often. Keep it close at hand, in the seat pocket in front of you.

➢ Use an eye shield—it will keep out the light and help you fall asleep more easily and sleep more soundly. Break it in by sleeping with it once at home prior to your trip. Adjust it so that it fits snugly over your eyes, but not so tight that you perspire. A bad fit may give you a headache and will flatten your hair! Using your eye shield is also an effective way to encourage a chatty neighbor to be quiet.

➢ Pack soft earplugs to mute airplane noise, the wailing of a baby, or the rock music seeping from your neighbor's CD player. Pellet-shaped foam earplugs may do the trick, but the soft silicone (or wax) variety that conform to the contours of your ear are the most effective.

➢ Bring socks in a carry-on bag. Wear them to keep your toes warm and to let your feet breathe.

➢ Consider using melatonin or a nonprescription sleeping aid such as Tylenol or Excedrin PM.

➢ Air circulated through airplane cabins is extremely dry. When traveling, carry lip balm and moisturizer in your carry-on bag

---

Melatonin has changed my life. I no longer suffer from jet lag. On either end of the trip I take 2.5 milligrams of the sublingual melatonin for three nights. I finish all my pre-bed rituals—bath or shower, vitamins, eye mask on and ear plugs in, get into bed, lights out, and then I take the pill. It's miraculous.

♦

—*Carol Benet, Ph.D., Belvedere, California*

to help prevent chapped lips and skin. Reapply throughout your plane ride.

➤ The effects of jet lag are generally more extreme when flying westbound. I use an all-natural homeopathic remedy called No Jet Lag, which is available at local health food stores, specialized travel stores, and markets like Trader Joe's.

➤ Try using different aromatherapy oils such as lavender, bergamot, neroli, or geranium, to help you relax during a long flight. To enliven a tired body after a flight, try essence of rosemary, clary sage, niaouli, or lemon.

➤ Many women experience irregular menstrual cycles because of jet lag, irregular eating and sleeping, and travel-related stress. On long flights, when long periods of sitting may aggravate premenstrual edema, try walking around the plane and exercising in your seat. Also consider reducing your salt intake the week before your period.

AIRPLANE STRETCHES

➤ Shoulder Shrug: Lift the top of your shoulders toward your ears until you feel mild tension in your shoulders and your neck. Hold your shoulders raised to your ears for five seconds, then relax and resume your normal posture. Do this two or three times every two hours.

➤ Back Twist: Interlace your fingers behind your head and raise your elbows straight out, parallel to the floor and level with your ears. Now pull your elbows backward and your shoulder blades toward one another. You'll feel a tension through your upper back and shoulder blades. Hold this position for ten seconds, then relax. Do it several times. This is a particularly good exercise to do when you've been sitting immobile and your shoulders and upper back are tense or tight.

➤ Head Roll: Begin with your head in a comfortable, aligned position. Slowly tilt your head to the left side to stretch the muscles on the side of your neck. Hold this stretch for ten to twenty seconds. You should feel a good, even stretch. Then tilt your head to the right side and stretch. Repeat this exercise two or three times on each side. Don't overdo it.

V
THE GUTSY DINER

There are three items that can provide nourishment and energy
for positive change: the air you breathe, the food you eat, and
the ideas you ponder. Travel can literally import a breath of fresh
air. . . . Eating new and different foods can nourish the spirit as
well as the body.

—*Karen Page, Becoming a Chef*

———

MY MOST IMPORTANT DINING tip is use common sense. Don't
pass on the pastries in France, the pizza in Chicago, the masala dosa
in India, or the clean food stalls in Thailand. Dining is a large part
of the discovery and pleasure of travel, but it can also cause some
of your worst memories.

Some people travel specifically to eat, and one of the best ways
to gain an understanding of another culture is through its cuisine.

I make a deal with myself. I can try anything that I have never tasted
before. I already know what chocolate, tiramisu, pâté, prime rib,
smoked salmon, etc. taste like. Foods that I've never tried before and
probably won't have the opportunity to sample at home are worth the
exception. I give myself permission to enjoy them wholeheartedly.
Everything tastes better without guilt.

♦

—*Laurie Armstrong, San Francisco, California*

The key to dining well and staying healthy is to eat the highest quality food possible. Only you can decide how bold you'll be, but it's part of the adventure of travel to try new things.

I may consider myself a risk taker, but when it comes to the equilibrium of my stomach, I am extremely cautious. Well, I did eat bamboo grubs in northern Thailand and yak eyeballs in Tibet, but both times they were well cooked and gave me less grief than eating a fast food hamburger in the USA. There are some gastronomic opportunities you just can't pass up.

Bon appétit!

TIPS

- Eat only thoroughly cooked food or fruits and vegetables you have peeled yourself. Remember: boil it, cook it, peel it—or forget it.

- Look at your meal carefully before you take the first bite. Never eat undercooked beef, pork, lamb, or poultry or raw eggs. Raw shellfish can be particularly dangerous to individuals who have liver disease or compromised immune systems.

- Do not eat or drink dairy products unless you know they have been pasteurized.

- Stay hydrated. Always carry a bottle of water with you when you travel and be sure to drink from it throughout the day. Do not wait for your body to tell you that you are thirsty—replenish continually.

> I relax my vegetarianism when I travel. It's much easier to make friends when I'm not trying to explain that I can't eat the foods they've kindly offered me.
>
> ◆
>
> —Jill Robinson, El Granada, California

> Never trust a culture that doesn't value chocolate.
>
> ◆
>
> —Betsa Marsh, Cincinnati, Ohio

- Carry a snack with you—you never know when you will need a little nourishment. Your growling stomach may wake you up in the middle of the night in a hotel with no room service or you could be stuck at a train station where everything is closed. Be prepared to nourish yourself immediately with nuts, dried fruit, or an energy bar.

- If you find yourself in a hole-in-the-wall restaurant where English is neither written nor spoken, just gesture to the waiter to follow you and walk right into the kitchen. Start pointing to this or that and make motions about how you want things cooked. The staff will love it. Ham it up. It is a great way to have a terrific meal and make friends.

- When dining at food stalls, be sure the meat is well cooked or the soup has been boiling for a while. Many of my seasoned travel friends say they wouldn't miss eating the mouthwatering local specialties available, at very reasonable prices, at food stalls. Others never go near them. As for me, I size up

---

You'll always remember the lavish dinner at a highly rated, upscale restaurant at your vacation destination—if for no other reason than the price. But picnics are another way to create indelible dining memories, and they stretch your travel budget at the same time. My travels have led me to memory-making picnics. On an unusually warm spring day, my husband, Jack, and I headed for the ruins of an ancient temple and theater in Sicily. There couldn't have been a more elegant setting for our simple lunch of crusty bread, salty prosciutto, cheese, sharp olives, and sparkling mineral water. Was our picnic inconsequential when compared to the breathtaking scenery? Not at all—it was a perfect complement, giving us a chance to linger and drink more deeply of the magnificent ancient theater.

◆

—*Marcia Schnedler, Little Rock, Arkansas*

the cleanliness of a stall, the clientele, the vendor, the food offered, and how it is cooked. I have had many fabulous meals and only a few painful memories from food stall experiences.

➢ Take along herbal tea. In many countries there are no decaffeinated beverages available.

➢ There is protocol for eating with your hands that must be learned from the local people, as it varies from country to country. Watch how the locals eat and ask if there is a certain etiquette. For example, in Malaysia it is considered bad manners if the food touches your hand too far up your finger, past the second knuckle. When in India, eat only using your right hand. The left hand is used for bodily hygiene and considered unclean.

> Don't pass up the opportunity to eat fabulous street food. Select a crowded, clean-looking stall. In Bali or Bangkok you may find everything from crickets to fried ants and snakes. Savor the initial "crunch." Remember, the story will be worth it when you get home.
>
> ◆
>
> —MB

➢ You may encounter different cultural challenges when dining on the road. A few you will want to remember:

Don't be surprised if you are a guest in a Muslim home and the hostess does not join you for dinner. Muslim women eat separately from the men.

If you are a guest out to dinner in Hong Kong, you can offer to pay even though it will probably not be accepted. Do not offer to split the bill, as this will result in loss of face for your host.

In Singapore, if you want to ensure good fortune, always make sure there is an even number of people present at the table.

In Taiwan, do not place your chopsticks parallel on top of your bowl or standing straight. This is bad luck and considered synonymous with a funereal ritual and death.

➤ If dining alone, why not ask to be seated at the counter? You can pick up a number of tips while watching the staff or chef at work. Check out the growing number of restaurants that offer a counter where you can cozy up to the kitchen and personally interact with a celebrity chef.

➤ Dining alone is an acquired skill. Take a book, postcards, or stationery with you so that you can enjoy your time in the restaurant.

➤ Ask your hotel concierge about restaurants that offer communal dining. From a small table of four to a large table of thirty, you never know with whom you will be seated. It is an opportunity to connect with other people—locals and travelers.

VI
ROMANCE ON THE ROAD

We travel, some of us forever, to seek other states,
other lives, other souls.
—*Anias Nin, The Diary of Anias Nin*

———

THERE IS SOMETHING EXTREMELY romantic about travel. The change of scenery often prompts you to step outside yourself and expand your normal boundaries. Maybe at home you wouldn't talk to a strange man or woman you met in a café and then later meet them for dinner. But when traveling, general rules are often pushed aside and new adventures take place. Wonderful things can happen when you meet exotic foreigners or other travelers. Only you can decide when or if to indulge in romance on the road. You could meet the love of your life, man or woman.

———

If it hadn't been for my incurable wanderlust, I never would have met my husband. If it hadn't been for the gentle charms of the Caribbean, I'd probably still be single. It is a wonderful story with a moral most profound. Sometimes you have to listen to your heart and not your head. The very things that attracted me to Bill for a shipboard romance were what seemed to make him unsuitable as a permanent mate. China blue eyes, sun-blond hair, an over-all tan, and a nomadic lifestyle? Hardly the stuff on which to base anything long-term, I kept telling myself. Thankfully, Bill was smarter about relationships than I.

♦

—*Judy Wade, Phoenix, Arizona*

I met my American husband in the Kathmandu Guesthouse in Nepal, and some of my friends have also met their spouses or significant others while traveling. Or they've had incredible experiences that they place very close to their heart.

Meet new people in public spaces. Be sure you know what the other person's intentions are, and also be clear about what you want out of the interaction. If you are interested in a short fling while traveling, be smart.

TIPS

- If you want to meet a like-minded companion or partner, participate in an organized tour with a special focus that appeals to you, such as an archeological dig, volunteer work, or an opera tour.

- Health spa retreats or meditation centers are good places to meet potential partners. People go to these places when they are making a life change and they are often more open and friendly. There is a time for group sharing and you talk about why you are there and what is going on in your life. Most people attend these sessions alone.

- Always watch your beverages while you are in a bar or restaurant to prevent tampering. The "date rape" drug, rohypnol (or roofie), may look as innocent as aspirin but is actually a very dangerous narcotic.

My philosophy has always been: Do what you love, follow your passion, and romance will follow. It worked for me.

♦

—MB

Make smart choices and use your common sense. Don't be paranoid, but be aware that bad things do happen, and protect yourself. In some countries accepting one or more drinks from an unknown man indicates your acceptance to sleep with him. Make your intentions clear.

♦

—MB

A potent tranquilizer similar in nature to Valium, but many times stronger, rohypnol produces a sedative effect, amnesia, muscle relaxation, and a slowing of psychomotor responses. Sedation occurs within twenty-to-thirty minutes. Go to bars with a buddy and keep an eye on each other.

➤ Be clear about what you want so you don't give mixed signals. If you want a fling, enjoy it. If you want something more lasting, examine your own feelings and ask yourself if his interest is genuine. Imagine introducing this person to friends and loved ones at home. Then trust your instincts.

➤ If you are the least bit inclined to find a lover, pack a supply of condoms. Remember, condoms bought in Bulgaria or India are not likely to be of the same quality as those bought at home. Some men, in many areas of the world, are not accustomed to discussing contraception and have negative feelings about using condoms, but you should insist on using them nonetheless.

> If you do have a one-night fling, be careful not to expose your money to that person. This happened to me: I got up and went to the bathroom. In the morning, after he was gone, I discovered he had stolen all the cash out of my purse. You never know who you can trust, especially if it is a guy you'll never see again.

♦

—Anonymous

➤ In numerous countries, such as Pakistan, Morocco, and India, up-scale hotels and tourist offices can arrange for a reliable male escort. He acts as your guide and bodyguard. This is not a cop-out. In some Muslim areas it is worth the minimal investment to enjoy touring without continual harassment.

HOW TO AVOID UNWANTED ADVANCES

➤ Dress conservatively and communicate an air of confidence and respectability.

➤ Walk with purpose.

➤ Consider wearing a wedding ring, if you don't already.

➤ Try to sit or stand next to other women or family groups in restaurants, on trains or buses, and in other public places.

IF YOU BEGIN TO GET PESTERED

➤ Completely ignore comments, catcalls, and whistles.

➤ Avoid all eye contact.

➤ Listen to your inner voice. If you are uncomfortable, get out of the situation immediately.

➤ If the pestering turns nasty, use forceful resistance: scream, fight, and flee! Research shows that rapists often seek to feel power and control over a weaker person. Your best defense is to resist and flee.

➤ In crowded environments like buses, men may harass you by pressing themselves against you. Don't let them get away with it. If the advance is especially ugly—suppose he presses his genitals against you—plant your elbow in his mouth, then scream at him (not swearing) in English with an air of great indignation.

➤ There is power in vocal embarrassment. I have found that many men are shamed by a verbal, loud woman admonishing them in public. Also shame them by shaking your finger in their faces. Even if the crowd doesn't understand your words, they will understand your indignation and gestures. Most sleazy men do not want public attention.

I was free and single when I was traveling so my experiences of foreign cultures were sometimes enhanced by my encounters with foreign men. I considered myself fairly sophisticated and savvy, but in retrospect I was rather naïve about my involvements—or maybe I was just hopelessly romantic. My adventures tended to obscure the reality that, as a Western woman, I've come to expect a certain level of respect and attentiveness that often wasn't granted by men of non-Western cultures. Ultimately, I realized (after many heartaches and disappointments) that I could never get what I needed from a relationship that sprang from fantasy to begin with.

◆

—*Kennerly Clay, Philadelphia, Pennsylvania*

VII
Budget and Money Matters

Take half the clothes and twice the money.
—*MaryBeth Bond*

———————

ALTHOUGH I HAVE BEEN asked dozens of times what it cost me to travel around the world for a year, it is almost impossible for me to say what it will cost you to stay for a month in Asia or two weeks in Europe. What you will spend depends on where you stay, where and what you eat, how you travel (plane, train, bus, rental car, on foot or bike), and how fast you travel. One person who travels twice as fast as another will spend a great deal more. Transportation, transfers in and out of cities, and lodging are a large percentage of a budget. A week lying on the beach in southern Thailand watching the waves roll in brings down your daily costs. If you stay in luxury hotels, fly everywhere, or see a lot of countries in a very short time you can spend a lot of money.

I spent under $5,000 to travel for a year, spending most of that time in Southeast Asia. That included all of my airfare, food, gifts, communications home—everything. Perhaps I could have spent half this amount, but I didn't want to scrimp and stay in dormitories or the cheapest hotels, always travel second class on trains, and learn to exist on rice and tea. I splurged to fly to Sri Lanka and the Maldives (where I went scuba diving . . . talk about expensive), and I enjoyed the old-fashioned Raj-style luxury of India's charming Maharaja Palace hotels. Remember that, most times, you will get what you pay for and many times its worth in unique experiences by paying a little more.

If you are traveling independently and are not going to one location (such as a condo in Hawaii), the best way to figure out a budget for yourself is to buy a good guidebook or go online and study it. Spend some time in a specialized travel bookstore sifting through the guides available for your destination. You can learn a great deal about the average prices for lodging, food, transportation, and entertainment in this way.

Unless you have a generous budget for your travels, choose your activities and countries carefully. Many areas of Asia (Nepal, India, Indonesia, Thailand, parts of China) and South America (Peru, Ecuador) are not only inexpensive areas to travel, they are also very welcoming to women. The longer you are gone from home, the lower your per diem will be. If you have the time, plan on staying in one area for a week or more. You will meet more local people as well as experienced travelers and learn where to eat, what to do, and where to stay.

TIPS

➢ Budget killers include not shopping around for your plane tickets; using taxis excessively; eating out all the time; staying at international chain hotels. When in doubt, ask other

---

Traveling overseas recently, I have noticed that many merchants ask me if I would like to have my credit card bill converted from the local currency (Euros, pounds, Argentine pesos, etc.) into dollars on the spot. It seems like they are offering you a nice service, when in fact, it's a money making scheme for them and costly for me. They set the exchange rate five or six cents more per dollar than the official bank rate and they keep the difference as a "service fee." To avoid these extra charges, read the fine print on the sales invoice, which will say that you agree to have your charge converted to dollars. Tell the merchant you do not want this service and refuse to sign.

—*MB*

---

travelers (before and during your trip) for their budget, lodging, and restaurant tips.

➤ You can save a lot of money by planning in advance. Consider alternative accommodations. For example, if you have done your research about Ireland, you will have learned about all the bed-and-breakfasts in the country. Not only are they much less expensive than staying in a hotel, they offer a huge breakfast, warm hospitality, and a chance to meet the people, not just see the sights. I have stayed in bed-and-breakfasts in the USA (even in Los Angeles!) to cut costs and add charm and intimacy to my travels.

➤ Ask the locals where they eat out. Leave the tourist areas of a city to find less expensive restaurants in more residential neighborhoods.

➤ Don't buy a whole new wardrobe for your trip prior to departure. Keep your pretrip shopping to a minimum. Buy what you need as you travel.

➤ When making reservations for car rental, accommodations, or miscellaneous tickets, always mention your membership in an organization—the American Association of Retired

I travel with a debit card, and two credit cards: It is cheaper and easier to use a debit card to get cash than to hassle with traveler's checks or cash and you get the best bank exchange rate. When you use a debit card you are typically charged a lower transaction fee than if you use your credit card. Contact your credit and debit card companies before you leave to notify them of the countries you will be visiting. They will make a note of where you'll be using your cards to charge and draw money from your account. Banks will close an account if they see a lot of activity in a foreign country and don't have prior information about your travel plans. It happened to me in Budapest and it was a big hassle to open my account again.

—MB

Persons (AARP), AAA—or affiliation to an academic institution. Often discounts are available for the asking.

- ➤ If you are staying at an establishment for a long time, or will be returning often, meet with the management and negotiate a special rate.

- ➤ Make a double-sided photocopy of your credit cards, ATM card and passport. Scan them and attach to an email to yourself.

- ➤ Play purchasing exercises with yourself while window-shopping to build your sense of the local currency—when you are ready to step into the store or stall, you will be better prepared to bargain. Memorize a currency "ladder" if you find it helps, e.g., how many rupees constitute $5, $10, $50? If you have a spending limit for a certain item, keep that number in mind in the foreign currency, not just in dollars.

- ➤ Protect your valuables. All of your important documents and money should be worn on your body. Your purse or shoulder bag should have enclosures like zippers or Velcro. Consider comfortable money belt or neck pouch. When the shoeshine boy and his buddies robbed a friend in Rio, they snatched the bills he took out of his trouser pocket and ran. They got $14. He had another $50 inside his sock and clothing. Only pull out small amounts of money at a time.

- ➤ Consider staying in a youth hostel. They are safe, friendly, people-oriented places filled with other budget-minded, adventurous travelers. There are over 5,000 hostels in 70 countries, including 150 in the USA. Not only do hostels offer extensive information about what to do locally, you will meet people who have already been where you may want to go and can give you the inside scoop on the good places to see, eat, and shop. Some hostels offer bicycle, canoe, or kayak rentals.

- ➤ These days YMCAs aren't just for young Christian men. There are branches in many major cities throughout the world, such as Hong Kong and New Delhi, that are safe and well located. You can make a reservation with a phone call and a credit card. If you don't like the accommodations or location, you can move after the first night. Be careful that the facility is not located in an unsafe neighborhood.

> If you travel in and out of major cities, use ATM withdrawals and credit card advances. If you'll be in remote areas for long periods of time, consider taking more cash.

> The best exchange rate you will find is through ATMs because they provide local currency (debiting your bank account at home). They give you the wholesale exchange rate and this can be from 5 to 10 percent higher than you get at hotels or exchange offices! Check with your bank about how to access your account overseas.

Keep $20 in small bills tucked away at all times. You may be leaving a country and find out there is a departure tax or if you need a tip upon arriving in a new country. This will save you from having to stand in line to get local currency.

◆

—MB

For the past decade, my friend Renae and I have left husband (hers), children (hers and mine), and, most recently, our grandchildren at home for destinations overseas. This past spring, our plans were to see how inexpensively we could travel in England and Scotland and at the same time do everything that excites us: go to the theater, see old friends, find the finest gardens, visit museums and art galleries. We wondered, as well, just how flexible and adaptable we really were, how well we'd cope with the unknown. So both of us decided that nothing less than staying at youth hostels would do. On the cheap, we concurred, is not just for the young! Would we do it again? Yes!

◆

—Rachel Pollack, Denver, Colorado

When traveling to developing countries, make sure that your bills are crisp and clean. Twice, once in Africa and once in Asia, banks refused to take my large bills because they had ink marks and they were dirty. Many shopkeepers will also refuse soiled or marked bills.

♦

—MB

➤ Guard your PINs carefully, whether they are for your ATM card or your telephone credit card. Stand close to the phone when dialing and punching in your number. Phone card thieves work public places with binoculars.

➤ Financial institutions may have restrictions on daily withdrawals that apply even when you are in another country. Check with your bank to find out how much you can take out each day.

➤ Before returning to the USA, convert all of your foreign coins and bills into U.S. dollars at the airport. Banks and exchange offices in the U.S. only accept bills and charge a hefty fee. Last summer I returned from Canada with $10 in Canadian bills. The fee to convert them to U.S. currency was $5. If you plan to return to that country again soon, you may be better off just holding on to the currency.

VIII
BARGAINING AND TIPPING

Bargaining is a game around the world—a game of wit and skill and words. Bring your best poker face, and prepare for fearless entertainment.

—*Kathy Borrus, The Fearless Shopper*

———

WANDERING THROUGH BAZAARS AND markets looking for local handicrafts is great fun. I use different negotiating styles with different vendors, rickshaw drivers, or cabbies and in different situations. Some travelers find bargaining humiliating, while others revel in it. It can be an unexpected source of local information and even friendship. When I find haggling with street vendors degrading, I give in or don't buy.

Once I fell in love with a beautiful jade disk necklace in the old town in Hanoi. I saw it in the glass cases of several shops before I asked the price and began to compare the workmanship on the hand-tooled silver casing. When I finally found a shop with several nice ones, I began to bargain. From the very beginning, I should have realized I had met my match, laughed, and given up. But I didn't. The Vietnamese woman, about my age, grew tired of my negotiating. She appealed to my husband and to our guide, and finally, with an air of indignation after my last offer, she bellowed, "Lady you cheap!" It is a funny story to tell now but, at the time, I was humiliated. I paid her asking price and hurried off. In the end, we were both losers, because I was planning to buy three necklaces instead of one. I smile and think of her every time I wear my "Lady You Cheap" necklace. She taught me an important lesson—pay the higher price and get what you want.

A friend of mine once bargained for a set of silver pony bells in a Tibetan town, but the old man offering them was absolutely unyielding in his price: $50 U.S. This seemed very high given the other goods and prices being offered at the market, and so my friend went home without the bells. Eight years later he reports that every Christmas he thinks wistfully of those bells as he puts up decorations. He realized that the bells may well have had a history for the old man, who was reluctant to part with them unless he got a very good price. Remember that the worth of something lies not in what is paid for the item, but what it means in your heart and life.

BARGAINING TIPS

➤ Before you begin bargaining, decide if you really want to buy the item. Do not waste your time or the salesperson's.

➤ Decide the top price you are willing to pay and know what that amount is in the local currency. Travel with a pocket calculator and use it to figure out the exchange rate before you pass through the doors of temptation.

➤ Eye contact with a shopkeeper will lead to a conversation. If you look them in the eyes, it can lead to a string of questions and it may be difficult to extricate yourself from the conversation without feeling rude.

➤ Watch out for engaging come-ons, such as this summons by a leather merchant in Antalya, Turkey, "Madame, I have everything you want."

Many people will ask you for money. Try to avoid giving money, especially to beggars on the street. In developing countries, they are often professionals. Be careful whom you give to. Not only will you burn out if you are cheated, but you may turn proud people into beggars. You will often know when people really need it.

♦

—*Olga Murray,*
Sausalito, California

Shopkeepers can be humorous and talented manipulators and will play on your sense of politeness. Only enter stores that you want to, and walk by those that you do not wish to enter—no matter how much the salesperson chides you.

➢ Occasionally accept offers of hospitality. I sipped a hot cup of apple tea in a spice market in Marmaris, Turkey, and heard all about a merchant's family and spice business. I did purchase spices from him, and even if I overpaid a little, it was worth it because I have the memory of the time spent with him in his shop.

➢ Avoid asking the price right away. In fact, look disinterested in the item you would like to buy. When you ask the price, if it is above what you had decided you would pay for such an item, leave. After this tactic, the merchant will usually approach you with a better price. Let the bargaining begin.

➢ Negotiations take time. Chat and have fun with it. Remember, it's all a dance and you will know when you are comfortable buying the item or walking away.

➢ Bargaining will vary from country to country. In India, for example, the first counteroffer can be 40 percent of the asking price and hopefully you can meet in the middle. In Turkey, however, you may only bargain for a ten or fifteen percent reduction. Ask the hotel manager, taxi driver, tour guide, or a local what they consider the local bargaining rules to be.

➢ Communicate shipping and payment arrangements early in the negotiations. If you are paying by credit card, the price may be higher. If you pay in cash, see what kind of discount this will add. If shipping

> Enjoy your new purchase and the relationship you made with the merchant. Don't look at the price of the same item later in the market, as it may only upset you. Be happy with the item and the experience.
>
>
>
> —MB

an item, make sure that you agree upon shipping method and time frame.

➤ If you are interested in buying more than one item, use that information as a bargaining tool for a larger discount.

➤ If you can afford the item, don't haggle over pennies or even dollars. Consider the merchant's lifestyle. The extra income could make a big difference in his or her life—if it won't impact your own, then pay a little more.

➤ Even if you end up not purchasing an item you have been bargaining for, be pleasant and leave the merchant on good terms.

➤ Contrary to popular wisdom, duty-free shops are not always filled with bargains. International passengers do not have to pay local taxes since they are exiting the country with the items, but sometimes merchants mark up prices to take advantage of a captive audience. If you have done your research and know what you are looking for, then there are bargains to be had.

TIPPING GUIDELINES

➤ There is no worldwide standard for tipping for services, but here is my rule of thumb: Never tip less than the price of a beer in the local currency.

➤ What might be viewed as a discretionary tip in our culture may be a necessary bribe for basic services in another. For example, in India tipping is a way of getting things accomplished. I have discovered that in some countries you must tip restroom attendants to receive a paper towel or toilet paper. If you don't tip them, they may follow you with a stream of insults.

➤ In addition to giving a monetary tip to someone like your guide, with whom you have spent several days, add something that will be meaningful to him or her. After climbing

Mount Kilimanjaro, my husband and I tipped our guide in cash and gave him our daypack. He was absolutely overjoyed with it because such packs were unavailable in Tanzania.

> ➤ If a taxi does not have a working meter, or the driver won't use one, avoid hassles or misunderstandings at the end of your taxi journey by negotiating the fare prior to entering the cab. Have a piece of paper available and insist he write the amount on it. Then be prepared for him to make one last effort for more money before you get out.

> ➤ In some cultures tipping is not customary or recommended. In Singapore it is officially discouraged and in Japan it is virtually unknown. In other cultures the service charge or gratuity is included in every bill. Ask a local person about the tipping customs of the country you are visiting.

> ➤ If tips are automatically included in a bill it is not necessary to leave more, but it may be customary to leave a small amount in cash. For example, in good Parisian restaurants the French leave an additional 5 percent on the table.

> ➤ Be careful when you sign your credit card charge form. Most receipts have a separate box for the gratuity. If there is no tip box on the form, ask the waiter how to include it in the charge.

> ➤ Some unscrupulous restaurant personnel have been known to write the total amount of the bill, including a predetermined

---

If you don't bargain, what is the worst thing that can happen? You might pay a little more than you would have if you'd haggled; a merchant in a developing country you don't know will gloat over hoodwinking a naïve tourist—but you'll end up with the object you wanted to have and maintain a mood you also wanted to keep.

♦

—Claire Walter, Boulder, Colorado

tip and service charge, in the top box of the charge slip. They leave the "tip" and "total" boxes empty and fill in an additional tip and new total after you have signed the bill. Ask if the tip is included and if it is, rewrite the total at the bottom before signing.

IX
Comfort on the Road

Up in the air you breathed easily, drawing in a vital assurance and
lightness of heart. In the highlands you woke up in the morning
and thought: Here I am, where I ought to be.

—*Isak Dinesen, Out of Africa*

WHETHER YOU ARE STRESSED out because of transportation
hassles—airline delays, cancelled flights, missed trains—or you
need a way to get back in touch with yourself when you are feeling swept away, rituals are simply something that you do to feel
comfortable and more in control.

There are many times when you may need a ritual to reduce
stress and clear a way for you to enjoy your destination. Maybe you
are on a business trip and you simply need to do something that will
make you feel like you have a life outside of work. The following
rituals are small things you can do to retreat from your travel life
and focus on yourself.

It's important to take care of yourself while you travel. Next
time you travel and are feeling frustrated or overwhelmed, breathe
deeply and try one of the following exercises.

RELAXING RITUALS

➢ Start every day with a good breakfast, exercise (even if you only
stretch or walk for fifteen minutes), and drink plenty of water
to prevent dehydration and periods of afternoon low energy.

➢ Put on comfortable clothes and stretch. Start with your neck
and work your way through your whole body.

- ➤ Meditate. Focus on your breath and empty your mind of all of the thoughts that are racing around. This will enhance your pleasure of what's to come.

- ➤ Listen to music.

- ➤ Take a shower and stand still for a minute to feel the warm water trickling from your head down to your toes. Imagine your discomfort and tension being washed away, leaving you cleansed and refreshed.

- ➤ Leave your lodging and find somewhere outdoors to sit. Wander through a park, watch the locals from afar, or stare at the moon. Just be still and let the world pass around you.

> While traveling, I set aside time each day to write in my journal. What are five new things I saw today? Whom did I meet? How do I feel? It slows me down to notice the details of my journey, so I can savor the people, the sights, the food, my inner landscape. It helps me realize that my travels are not just about viewing the world, they're about truly seeing myself.
>
> ♦
>
> —Lisa Bach, Oakland, California

- ➤ Practice reflexology. Give your ear a massage and it will be like you had a full body message. There are over a hundred reflexology energy points located in your ears that are connected to different organs and body parts.

- ➤ Read a good book. Download or bring along a couple of paperbacks to read along the way. When you finish one, exchange it with another traveler.

MAKE YOUR HOTEL ROOM A HOME AWAY FROM HOME

- ➤ So many people complain about their hotel rooms—why not make improvements to them instead? Even if you are only staying for a couple of nights, try to make it feel as much like home as possible.

- Unpack your suitcases and put them away. Do not live out of the suitcases. If you are used to having a sock and underwear drawer, then unpack and create the same organization.

- Place a photo of your family or friends on the bedside table.

- If you are used to having flowers in your home, go to a local florist and get yourself a small bouquet to keep in your room. Or keep the flower from a room-service cart for your room.

- Move the desk to where it is most comfortable for you to work. If you like to have a view or more natural sunlight when you read or write, move the desk near the window.

- When you buy presents for friends and family, have them gift-wrapped with a pretty ribbon. Leave these gifts out in your hotel room for a festive look and a connection to home.

- Hide all of the hotel's promotional reading material and place your magazines or books in their place.

When all else fails, throw money at it. If you're delayed three hours at an airport, don't fret in the crowded waiting area, find the best restaurant and splurge on a good meal.

♦

—Scottie Held, Bolton, Massachusetts

X

THE BUSINESS TRAVELER

Enjoy the place you are visiting. Don't work all the time.
—Anonymous Frequent Flyer

———————

TRAVEL IS A WONDERFUL perk for many working women, although after the first few trips many individuals do not find it fun or glamorous anymore. It adds stress and consumes personal time we might rather spend with friends and family. Can we learn ways to be smart business travelers? Frequent flyers whose jobs demand that they travel will tell you "Yes." They live on airplanes, at airports, in hotels, driving countless miles in rental cars.

Here are some basic, road-tested tips to help make your business travel easier.

> ———————
>
> I always travel with a Pashmina shawl, it can be used as a coat, a sweater, a scarf, a pillow, a belt, or even a beach cover-up.
>
> ♦
>
> *—Gail Krauss,*
> *Vermilion, Ohio*

TIPS

➤ Record all of your confirmation numbers—hotel, car rental, flight information, etc.—on your smart phone. I have jotted down these vital numbers on my airline ticket jacket and later discovered that an efficient ticket agent threw it away and gave me a clean one. If your reservation is lost or the computer is down, you will be prepared. If your flights are delayed, you'll need to call ahead to confirm a late arrival;

if you bring the vital phone and confirmation numbers with you, handling the situation will be a breeze.

➢ Pack lightly, bringing only carry-on luggage if possible. Pack the least amount of clothes you think you can survive on. You can wear the same mix-and-match outfits day after day. Leave room in your bag for shopping treasures you can't resist along the way.

➢ How many shoes does the gutsy business traveler pack? Too many, usually! If the shoe fits, wear it, don't carry it. Wear the shoes you'll need for business and pack one pair of athletic shoes for walking, jogging, or informal occasions.

➢ Pack dark clothes. They don't show spots or dirt and work for most situations.

➢ If you need to be dressed in business attire at your meeting, be sure to wear it on the plane or carry it with you; if your luggage is delayed or lost, you won't be forced to shop.

➢ Sleep smart. Dark circles under your eyes aren't good for business. Carry eye shields and earplugs to counter jet lag or a poor night's sleep in a strange hotel room. Silicone earplugs work best, muting noise, snoring, and annoying chatty airline neighbors. Also, invest in a blow-up pillow to help you sleep soundly on the plane—it will also prevent your hair from being flattened as you sleep, and your neck from getting a crick.

➢ Ask for a hotel room away from the ice machine, elevator, and on the quiet side of the building. It can make a huge difference for your sleep that night and your mood the next day.

I have a cosmetic bag pre-packed with travel size items that I know I always need when I'm traveling for business. I never have to worry about getting somewhere and not having a toothbrush, toothpaste, shampoo, conditioner, Q-tips, deodorant, etc. It's a great relief to simply grab the kit and go.

◆

—Kim Arnone, Berkeley, California

- Hotel alarm clocks and wake-up services can be unreliable. Use the alarm on your cell phone.

- Carry food rations. Airlines offer little more than the tiny, salty servings of peanuts or pretzels for many flights. If your flight is delayed or has mechanical problems, you may spend hours on the runway or circling in the air while your stomach is screaming.

- Before driving off the lot at the rental car agency, walk around the vehicle to check for dents or other damage. Insist that everything be verified in writing by the rental agent and keep a copy.

- If you must leave valuables or luggage in your vehicle, be sure they are locked in the trunk or well hidden.

- Pack more than double the number of business cards you think you will need. Handing someone your card makes a professional statement and immediately establishes your credibility.

- Have your business information printed on the reverse side of your cards in the language of the country where you will be doing business.

- If you are doing business in Asia, present your business card with both hands. After you accept your colleague's card, carefully and respectfully store it in a good place. Don't just slip it into your back pocket.

- The concierge at your international hotel is your best source of local information and help.

- How much money do you need? With a debit card or

Be prepared for the unexpected. Food spills can happen on your clothes anytime and anywhere—in the driver's seat of a car, on the plane, or during a business lunch. Pack an instant stain remover in your purse for quick cleanup. A portable stain removing pen is designed to remove most fresh food and drink stains like coffee, ketchup, barbeque sauce, soy sauce, soda, and tomato juice.

♦

—*MB*

major credit card, you can obtain cash in almost every major city in the world. If you are prone to forgetting your PIN number at home, then write down a coded version in the back of your passport.

➤ Laptop computers, smart phones and Ipads have become popular items for theft. Stay on the alert, especially when passing through security X-ray machines. A thief watches you place your electronics on the conveyer belt of the X-ray machine, then cuts in line in front of you and sets off the metal detector. While you are delayed, your gear passes through the machine and a second thief snatches it and quickly disappears. Another technique involves someone spilling coffee or ketchup on you. When you stop and put down your bags to clean it off, be sure your laptop is secured firmly between your legs.

➤ Mix pleasure with your business. When your time is limited, a tour can help you see the best of what the city has to offer and can be a great way to treat a client.

Before I pack my jewelry, whether it is expensive (or expensive looking), I ask myself if it will fit in or if it will be appropriate in a business setting. In Paris, probably; in Quito, probably not. In some cities, wearing expensive jewelry is an invitation to mugging. Consider the context of where you are going and what you will be doing.

—*MB*

XI
FIRST-TIME TRAVELERS

A journey of a thousand miles musts begin with a single step.

—Lao Tzu

━━━━━━

ALL OVER THE COUNTRY, women of all ages have asked me to give them some words of encouragement to help them step out the door. Some ask, "Do you think I should go?" I tell them "Yes." To boost my self-confidence before I took off on my journey around the world, this is what I did: Every morning as I looked into my mirror, I asked myself, What's holding you back? What is the worst that could happen? How will you feel about yourself in six months or a year if you don't fulfill your dream? Look at everything you have already accomplished. This is just one more little risk. You know that the first step is the hardest. So quit agonizing over the decision and just go!

> ━━━━━━
>
> I tell all young people: Travel now while your knees are good and before you settle down. People put off travel for many reasons, but you should do it while you are mobile, active, interested in meeting and learning about people.
>
> ◆
>
> *—Rosemary Gardner, Oakland, California*

TIPS

➤ Before you go, decide honestly what the most important goals are for your trip. Do you want to see lots of sights? Meet as many people as possible? Get to know yourself better? Begin learning a new language? You will be tempted by many choices, but having a clear idea in mind of what you really want from your journey will help you decide what to do and what to skip and you will return home feeling satisfied.

➤ Make a conscious decision about your preferred travel companions. Think through your goals and what you are willing to compromise. Do your homework. If you choose to join a group, call numerous tour operators, collect and read brochures, then decide if you prefer travel with a like-minded group or alone. One of your most important decisions will be who you travel with. Don't make this decision hastily.

➤ If you choose to travel independently, consider arranging a homestay at the beginning of your trip. It can be as simple as renting a room with a family or arranging an extended stay at a family guesthouse. See the Resources section for a list of organizations that arrange homestays.

> We all share a desire to fulfill our dreams, but few of us act on it. Over and over again women tell me that taking an adventure travel vacation was often the first time they acted on a totally new experience in their lives. For the first time they went somewhere alone, met new people, or learned about another culture. For the first time they experienced an active vacation and physically challenged themselves. They have all come away feeling a newfound and positive sense of self.

♦

—Susan Eckert,
Bozeman, Montana

➤ Make sure your baggage is properly routed at check-in. It is very easy for a tired airline employee to misroute a bag with the wrong destination tag. Learn the particular code for your destination.

➤ If your seatmate on an airplane, bus, or train is driving you nuts with nonstop talk, put on headphones, if you have them, smile, and turn your head away.

➤ Create cheat sheets for local lingo. It is important to be able to say a few rudimentary words in the local language, such as please, thank you, beautiful, spicy, not spicy, and delicious. To cheat easily and help you memorize the vocabulary, write basic words on a small sheet of paper or your arm for reference.

➤ When you first arrive in a new city, if you can, take a half-day tour to get oriented.

➤ Before heading out to explore a new city, pick up a business card from your hotel. It's easier than you think to get lost and forget your way back, and a card in your possession will tell taxi drivers or anyone you ask for directions where you want to go. This is particularly important in countries like Thailand, Japan, or China, where you may not be able to read the script and locals may not speak or read English.

Apply for a passport or check the one you have three to six months before your departure. Numerous countries do not allow entry with a passport considered "soon to expire" (within six months). Handle your passport and visa paperwork long before your departure to avoid paying huge surcharges for last minute services. You may need travel immunizations depending upon where you will be traveling. If they are required for entry into a country, you'll need an International Health Certificate to prove you've gotten all of them, and carry the certificate while traveling. Remember to start your travel immunizations early enough to finish the series of shots before traveling.

♦

—MB

➤ Establish routines. Connect to the place you're visiting by going to the same coffee shop every morning and reading the paper. Stroll along the river, waterfront, or town square each evening and you'll start to see familiar faces. It can help you feel a sense of belonging in a new location.

➤ Carry a small or medium-size backpack for all the things you'll need during the day: journal, camera, water bottle, sweater, guidebook. Select one with a sturdy zipper, several compartments, and padded shoulder straps.

➤ Last-minute purchases in the airport that make a difference: a pack of gum to relieve pressure in your ears, if needed, and for bad breath; postcards of your hometown to share or give away; snacks to stave off midnight hunger while you are adjusting to new mealtimes.

XII
THE STUDENT TRAVELER

Women who travel as I travel are dreamers.
Our lives seem to be lives of endless possibility.
—*Mary Morris, Nothing to Declare*

————

TODAY MORE AND MORE students are taking off for semesters abroad, for volunteer programs like Los Amigos or independently to travel through Europe, Asia, or south of the border.

I lived and attended university in Europe (Luxembourg and Paris) and had marvelous experiences. It was one of the best learning opportunities of my life. To be honest with you, however, my experiences also included sexual verbal harassment, unwanted touching (in crowded buses), inappropriate comments, crude propositions, and a man who exposed himself to me. I learned quickly how to avoid potentially compromising situations and how to dress appropriately.

I have spoken to numerous university organizations for students who are preparing to live or travel abroad. The college felt it was necessary because female students returned from their semesters abroad with negative experiences that could have been avoided. They realized how unprepared so many of their students were regarding the dress code, dating behavior, nightclub etiquette, and safety. Before your departure, it's helpful to understand the stereotypes many foreign men have.

Unfortunately, young North American women are often viewed as naïve, "loose," and craving sex (thanks to American media, television stereotypes, and to revealing fashions). Thus young American women are often targets for sexual come-ons.

In some countries women dress more conservatively than we do in North America. Learn about the acceptable women's dress code and "bar behavior" for the country you'll be visiting. Take note of the behavior and dress of young local women. Do they smile at strange men, accept drinks from strangers or show cleavage? What message do you project? Not all men have your best interests at heart. In some cultures a bare belly or tight t-shirt is offensive and may invite nasty advances from the men.

We're also more likely to be the victims of theft, so read on and learn how to protect yourself and your valuables. Pickpockets, scam artists, and smugglers are clever and experienced and usually work in crowded areas so stay alert and hide your valuables.

TIPS

➤ Are you traveling with friends? Spend part of the day on your own and meet up for dinner. That way, you'll get important time to yourself, have your own stories to tell, and remain appreciative of each others' company.

➤ Don't push your limits where there are no safety nets. For instance, are you an idealist? Prone to political activism? Keep in mind that many countries do not have the democratic liberties of the U.S., and that getting involved in the local politics of a foreign country can be quite dangerous. My advice: Don't. Better to save your hard-core activism for U.S. soil, where you know the rules, the consequences of breaking them, and where help is closer at hand if you need it.

➤ Make smart choices and use your common sense. Don't be paranoid, but be aware that bad things do happen—protect yourself by following your instincts.

➤ Most of the people who offer you food or drink are just being kind. However, the rare exception exists—drugging occasionally happens. Don't leave your drink unattended in bars, and exercise good judgment when accepting food or drink from people.

- Be aware of your vulnerabilities as a young woman on the road. For instance, in many countries, it is common for gigolos to prey on young female travelers. Don't be naïve about the intentions of foreign men.

- Are you in the mood for love? Make sure it's safe. AIDS is a growing crisis in many developing countries—ALWAYS use a condom.

- If you think you are pregnant, get a test. If it is positive, have a second test and then travel to a Western country (like Australia or England) or come home to deal with your options.

> Keep your important travel documents, like your passport and electronic ticket itinerary, in the same place, where it's easy to get to them.
>
> ◆
>
> —MB

- How do you know when you've overstayed your welcome at someone's house? Many cultural exchange programs impose a two-night minimum so you get to know your hosts, and your stay can last as long as it works for both parties. Leave before it is time.

- Stay flexible and remember that you can always come home. There's a lot of pressure to continue your travels, but if you're not enjoying yourself, if the trip is not what you expected, you can change your plans en route or come home. Sometimes just giving yourself permission to

> Always take your money with you when you leave your seat to go to the toilet in airplanes.
>
> ◆
>
> —MB

come home will clarify that you really want to continue traveling. Or you might realize you're just not ready for India yet, and that's okay too. Remember, being gutsy is about being true to yourself.

➤ Most students overseas don't wear baseball hats with logos, "I Love New York" t-shirts, or sweatshirts advertising their university's name. This type of clothing will make you stand out when you want to blend in. Also consider taking one nice outfit for nights out.

Leave your expensive or expensive-looking jewelry at home. You don't want a thief to yank it off your neck, wrist, or earlobes.

➤ Crowded buses or trains, train stations, and busy streets are areas where groping or thefts occur. Try to sit or stand next to other women or family groups in restaurants, on trains or buses, and in other public places. It is unlikely that you will be approached or harassed if you're in the company of other people. There is safety in numbers.

➤ Learn to look gutsy. Even if you feel a little frightened or intimidated, adopt a no nonsense, "don't f. . . . with me" attitude. Walk with purpose; throw your shoulders back, and chin up and you'll be less of a target for hustlers who prey on disoriented or timid-looking women. If you pretend you're gutsy, you may begin to feel gutsy, too.

>
> In all the Muslim countries in which I have traveled, I stood out as a foreign woman, even when I was modestly dressed. I learned to cover my arms and legs with loose, non-clinging clothing. I found it helpful to cover my hair in most Islamic countries and to avoid all eye contact with unknown males. All these precautions helped reduce the unwanted attention from men. When you visit mosques you will be required to cover your hair.
>
> ◆
>
> —MB

➤ Don't leave your street smarts at home, and listen to your inner voice. Trust your instincts. They are well-honed from living in the USA. If you feel something is off, wrong, strange—get out, move on, flee, scream, whatever is appropriate. Do it quickly.

➤ Women should follow simple dress guidelines for travel in Muslim countries. Many Muslim women aren't seen in public and live most of their lives inside, out of view of strange men. (Read *Palace Walk*, part of the Cairo Trilogy by Naguib Mahfouz).

➤ Safe bar behavior differs from country to country. What you can do comfortably in Australia you cannot do safely in Morocco. Ask local female students what's appropriate. In some countries accepting one or more drinks from an unknown man indicates your acceptance to sleep with him.

➤ Always go to a bar with a companion and promise you will leave together. Keep an eye on each other and don't go outside the bar for a smoke or a breath of fresh air without your buddy.

➤ When traveling overseas be wary of anyone who asks you to carry a package or drive a car across a border. Innocent young women are especially targeted to be couriers for drug dealers. The young man they meet may be charming and persuasive. Once a package or anything in the vehicle is in your possession, you become totally responsible for it. You will be guilty until proven innocent, assessed a huge fine, and may spend time in jails where the living conditions are barbaric. Even in Mexico, if you are convicted of possessing even small amounts of marijuana or cocaine, you'll go to jail.

➤ Your student ID (with a photo) will get you discounts in the USA and internationally so don't leave home without it. Many student travelers also purchase the ISIC (International Student Identity Card) for discounts on travel rates, accommodations, museums, cultural venues, entertainment, basic sickness and student travel insurance abroad, and cheap international phone calls.

➤ Stay in touch. While you're on the road—keep in touch with those you leave behind. Calm your concerned mom or dad.

They'll love to hear all about your experiences and to see up-to-date photos of you.

➤ Pack a small zip lock bag with photos of your friends and family. Include pictures of your home, a birthday party or family get together. When you stay in one place for a few nights, put the photos around your room to create a homey atmosphere filled with friends and loved ones. You'll also meet lots of wonderful people along the way who will want to know more about your life at home and who will enjoy seeing your pictures.

➤ Expect some loneliness or homesickness. It will come and go, like PMS. Don't cut your travels short unless you absolutely have to. Make sure you make the most of your time away. You'll miss friends and family loads, but you do go through phases and as long as you call or email them frequently they'll be okay . . . and so will you.

➤ Visit the local markets and bazaars for great bargains, colorful displays, and fun people-watching. Jump in and haggle with the vendors for the best price.

➤ To get beneath the surface of a culture, talk to the locals and live like them. Stay in a home, family-run guesthouse or couch surf. (See the resource section for organizations). Travel like the locals; walk, bike, take buses or trains. Get up early and go to the market or to a park to join an exercise group. In Hanoi

---

What happens if your passport or important documents are stolen or lost? Prepare for this possibility before your departure. Leave copies of your passport, drivers' license, credit and debit cards, and e?ticket itineraries with a family member or someone you can get in touch with easily who will not be traveling. Also scan and email copes to yourself. This way you have two backups.

—MB

I did Tai Chi every morning with the local senior citizens in a park. We all had a good laugh about my clumsiness.

➤ Take time to talk to local people. You can start with gestures and smiles. It helps if you can learn several words in their language. In my experience, the most important words are:

After studying in France and getting a taste of the lifestyle, culture and language, many Americans dream about returning to live in Paris or in an idyllic village somewhere, to write, hike, cycle, garden, and enjoy life with friends and family.

I spent three years studying on the Cote d'Azur, but especially loved la France profonde, far from the areas favored by most tourists. My understanding of French culture, architecture, literature, art, and cuisine improved over time. I also met a wonderful circle of friends who were painters, writers, sculptors, filmmakers, and artisans, who were living well, and able to focus on their passion, rather than their paycheck.

Years later, my American husband and I found a dilapidated manor house in a medieval village nestled between 1000-foot cliffs, with a stream out back and castle next door. We bought it, even though we lived on the Pacific Coast, 6,000 miles away. For over ten years, we've enjoyed living there, where our daughter was also born. We were ready (and crazy enough) to seize the moment, and embark on a new adventure.

Our French (and many expat) friends and neighbors do live well, many with a very modest income. What they have in abundance is time to *create*—whether it be a painting, a poem, a beautiful garden, a stone wall, a book of photographs, or an extraordinary meal. They understand the choices, and challenges, that come with such a lifestyle.

The manor is now a B&B, where we've hosted hundreds of guests, and dealt with masons, roofers, plumbers, electricians, and the typical quirks that come with a 400-year-old house. What an excellent adventure it continues to be and it all began as a student falling in love with France.

◆

—*Sarah Weldon, San Francisco Bay Area*

hello, thank you, beautiful, delicious, boy and girl. You can point to a child and say "beautiful" then add with a question in your voice; boy? girl? Or you may touch a woman's handicraft necklace or earrings and say, "beautiful." In Tibet I couldn't quite bring myself to say "delicious" about the yak eyeballs in the soup or the yak butter tea.

XIII
THE SOLO TRAVELER

Traveling alone is not lonely; it's an extremely powerful feeling,
very similar to love—it's that kind of strength. It's partly the joy of
total aloneness—not loneliness—of being part of the land, as far as
you can see and knowing there's nobody you need share it with.

—*Christina Dodwell, Travels with Pegasus*

WHEN I STARTED TRAVELING alone, at age twenty-nine, it was
not by choice. I couldn't find anyone to travel with me. I had two
options: stay at home and give up my dream, or go alone. So I swallowed hard, bit my lower lip, and told the world and myself that I
could do it. I would do it. I would go alone. I did. And I loved it! I
traveled solo for the next two years
around the world.

Starting out alone does not
mean staying alone. There are
many other fascinating people out
there traveling by themselves, just
like you. At times I would hook up
with a kindred spirit and we would
travel together for a few days, even
for a month. Many of these travel
companions are still close friends.
My decision to go alone was one
of the best choices of my life.

What's so great about it?
Solo travelers enjoy the freedom of making all the decisions,

I have many opportunities to
take my husband along on my
travels and often do. But when
I travel alone, it's an entirely
different trip. Instead of being
focused on the person with
you, you are more observant,
more attuned to every sound
and detail. And you are much
more likely to meet people.

♦

—*Kimberly Brown-Seely,
Pacific Northwest*

experience the world unfiltered by anyone else's perspective, live intensely, meet people more easily and are invited into their lives more readily, avoid difficult travel companions, and get in touch with themselves.

Now when I create the opportunity to travel alone, it is a self-indulgent luxury. If you give it a fair chance, you too will discover that solo travel is empowering, intense, and exhilarating.

Divorce or the death of a spouse or partner can leave an avid traveler faced with the same dilemma I had. Do you choose to stay immobilized? Can you find a new travel companion? Or should you go alone? Eventually you'll begin doing day trips alone. In time you may move on to overnights, then longer journeys, until you are surprised and pleased by how confident and happy you are traveling alone.

TIPS

➤ You can begin traveling solo at any age. Fortunate are the women who began traveling alone when they were young.

Everything was magnified by my being alone. In India, exploring a new city on foot, so pleasant in Europe, meant running the gauntlet: hawkers, beggars, insistent merchants came to me from everywhere, invading my per?sonal space. With a companion, such scenes might have been merely local color. A twosome, self-contained, has its own resources. Through conversation and feed-back, it can defuse the impact of the unfamiliar in a way that the solo traveler cannot. Alone and uninitiated, I felt like Snow White assaulted by Disney's animated trees. Every experience was intensely my own, undiluted by the connection to home that a familiar companion supplies. Occasionally I thought, no one on earth knows where I am. That one point held both the exhilaration and the vulnerability of traveling alone.

♦

—*Jo Broyles Yohay, New York City*

Often they tell me they never experienced any trepidation. For those of you who aren't too sure—try it. Don't let fear stop you. Other travelers on the road and local people will support you and you'll discover how much inner strength you possess.

➤ Consider taking a short trip first to see if you like traveling alone. Find a cute town close by and visit for the weekend. Bring something to read, a journal, and some good music. Explore your surroundings. Be aware of your solitude and how it feels to be on your own. Then, if you're ready, plan a more adventurous trip. It's O.K. to start small.

➤ Start smart. Even if you want to be unstructured, book at least the first night's accommodation in advance. It will be easier to feel comfortable and get your bearings.

➤ When you travel alone, you accept the responsibility to reach out, be extroverted, and strike up conversations with strangers. You'll find it is much easier to make new friends when you are alone. You are more approachable.

➤ Trust your intuition, no matter what. You will have many great opportunities to explore new places and meet exciting people. One of the best things about travel is being open to these experiences. Just pay attention to your gut when you

One of my most memorable encounters in Sri Lanka would not have occurred if I had not been alone and not accepted the kind offer of help from strangers. I was waiting at what I believed to be a bus stop when a man in a battered station wagon filled with cheerful kids stopped and offered me a ride. He informed me that where I was standing was not a bus stop. I accepted his offer because of the presence of his four children. His invitation for a ride to my guesthouse led to a dinner with his wife and a school-teacher, tours of the island, and a charming friendship.

♦

—MB

find yourself in a new situation. It will tell you when to go for it and when to get out. Always listen to your instincts and they will help keep you safe in the midst of your adventures.

➤ Women traveling alone share similar concerns about loneliness, safety, harassment, illness, and accidents. Don't worry. Going alone is not necessarily more dangerous than traveling with a companion—it just requires extra awareness. You will discover how fine-tuned your survival instincts are. Most countries in the world are not as violent or dangerous as our own. If you need help, ask for it.

➤ Don't travel alone into the backcountry—make sure at least one or two others accompany you. A backcountry injury without someone to help can pose a life-or-death situation.

➤ Buy or download popular guidebooks. The accommodations and restaurants listed will be full of other independent travelers, so you'll have plenty of opportunities to hook up with a variety of people. You may find yourself exploring the bazaar or eating a meal with your new friends, or you might even travel for a time together. Use your guidebook as an indication of things to see and where to start your journey, then travel farther off the beaten path.

> Every time we set foot on our own as solo travelers, we shave off the edge of oddness and anomaly. We are seen enjoying ourselves, taking care of ourselves. We pave the way for normalcy someday for all those women peeking out from kitchen curtains and behind veils.
>
> ◆
>
> —*Joan Medhurst, Alameda, California*

➤ Don't isolate yourself in a hotel or rental car. It's much easier to meet people if you are out and about with locals and other travelers. Use public transportation and stay in hostels, local homes, or bed-and-breakfasts. You will probably meet so many people that you just might yearn for some time alone!

- Check out the meeting places for independent travelers. Some guidebooks (such as the Lonely Planet series) will list them. Many cities have well-known meccas for independent travelers, with bulletin boards and unique calendars of local events. These are treasure troves of inexpensive tours, travel companions or rides wanted, free or almost-free local lectures, and social gatherings, that you can join. A morning jog with the running group "Hash House Harriers" in Singapore or Kathmandu can lead to local friends and social invitations. My handwritten note posted on a message board on a tree in the café courtyard of the Old Stanley Hotel in Nairobi led to a safari with wonderful people and dynamic friendships.

- Take advantage of your solo status and be willing to change your plans. One of the greatest things about traveling alone is that you get to do whatever you want to do, all the time. Make an impromptu side trip to the beach. Add an entire country to your anticipated itinerary. Stay in bed all morning on a rainy day. Revel in the joy of not having to compromise.

- Treat yourself to small luxuries like high tea at an elegant hotel or a manicure.

- When graciously offered, accept spontaneous invitations and hospitality, especially from women or families. Be careful, however, not to overstay your welcome or create a hardship for the family.

- How do you handle eating alone in a restaurant? Choose a bistro, café, or lively place. Go prepared with reading and writing materials—postcards, letters, and your journal. Comfortably dining alone is a learned skill. Eventually you'll find yourself enjoying watching people and eavesdropping. And you won't always stay alone after being seated in a restaurant. I have often been invited to join other travelers or vice versa.

- Don't be afraid to eavesdrop. It's a great way to identify interesting people with whom you might share something in common. Find a sneaky way to join the conversation.

FOR OVERCOMING THAT
LONELY FEELING

I am often asked, "Do you ever get lonely, and what do you do about it?" I am surprised by how rarely I do get lonely.

To minimize your uncomfortable feelings, keep in mind that loneliness is a bit like PMS—predictable, irritating, and temporary.

➢ Different moments in your trip will require different approaches to coping with loneliness. Sometimes it's important not to sink into your loneliness. To counter loneliness, stay active. Take a walk in a park, eat in lively, crowded restaurants, initiate conversations with strangers, and shop for gifts for your friends and family. Other times giving in to your mood is the best possible medicine. At times like this, I become reclusive, reading, listening to music, writing in my journal or to friends and family.

> I missed meeting a friend at the Lisbon train station and discovered the world of solo travel. Traveling alone, I think the smells are sharper, the sounds more distinct, the flavors more powerful, and the people much friendlier.
>
> ◆
>
> —*Kari Bodnarchuk,*
> *Bellingham, Washington*

➢ When you're feeling low, I don't recommend calling home. It can make you feel worse. But writing postcards or sending a text or email is uplifting.

➢ Take care of yourself. When I start to feel lonely, it's often because I haven't eaten or slept enough or I've had too much caffeine. If I stay well fed, fit, and rested, then depression, loneliness, and illness are usually avoided.

➢ Treat yourself. I love to pamper myself with a hot bubble bath, new music or new books, or have a massage or manicure. In India and Thailand I bought garlands of gardenias and richly fragrant flowers for my room. In Chicago I got

> Recognize the difference between solitude and loneliness. I made the choice to be alone and I like my own company. Now I cherish my time alone and accept the lonely moments. They never last long. They come and go, just like at home.

◆

—MB

dressed up and went to a posh hotel for a drink and hours of people watching.

➤ Write in a journal. When you find yourself missing your best friend at home, write down everything you want to tell her or him in your journal. Don't just put down what you saw that day—include how you're feeling about yourself and your trip. If you want to go home, write about it! Periodically read back over your journal and see how your journey is unfolding. Take yourself out to dinner when you realize how fabulous you are!

> Alone we can afford to be wholly whatever we are and to feel whatever we feel absolutely.
>
> ◆
>
> —May Sarton, Poet

XIV
TRAVEL COMPANIONS

One of the great things about travel is you
find out how many good, kind people there are.

—*Edith Wharton*

———

FOR MANY WOMEN, TRAVELING with other women takes the fear out of seeing the world. Women always ask how they can meet other women travel companions. They are single, divorced, or widowed; their husbands aren't interested in travel; or their friends won't travel without their husbands. Now more than ever women are interested in finding other women to travel with.

I encourage women to meet other women for the sole purpose of travel. Find someone who shares your passion for wandering the globe or for weekend getaways. Or meet someone local who has similar interests—for example, photography—and go on a photography travel expedition together. There are many travel companies that specialize in planning trips specifically for women (see the Resources section for more information). These trips are a lot of fun and chances are you will meet others that you might want to travel with in the future.

> A different kind of bonding unfolds on an all-women trip. Last spring I traveled for twelve days in France with seven women I didn't know. Traveling with women is a different and wonderful kind of fun. So if you're married and your husband doesn't like to travel, leave him at home. He'll be there when you get back.
>
> ◆
>
> —*MB*

New friendships are formed on the road, and life-long relationships deepened. A getaway with your girlfriends can be a wonderful thing, one that will remind you why you've been friends for so long. It gives you a chance to spend quality time together and gives you an increased comfort level while traveling. When you travel with other women, be open to self-discovery and self-revelation. Get to know the women you are traveling with and share your life experiences with them. This part of the journey holds wonderful possibilities. Enjoy your time bonding with the other women on the trip, and be open to meeting even more women in the destinations to which you are traveling.

TIPS

➢ Before you and your travel companions leave, acknowledge that problems may arise and discuss how you will deal with them. Be honest about your "hot buttons" (people being bossy, chronic lateness) and agree to be sensitive to each other's particular needs. Be open when something is bothering you and address it immediately. Talk issues through and don't let them fester. Then let them go and enjoy your trip.

➢ It's always good to set boundaries before you go. If you know that you need personal quiet time each day, then be sure to articulate this to your travel partner. That way she won't take it personally and will know that you simply need your space. See "Roommate Checklist" below for more information.

➢ Don't assume that you can borrow your travel partner's make-up, brush, shampoo, conditioner, toothpaste, or clothes. Just because you are traveling together, that doesn't mean her items are up for grab. Be respectful and ask permission if you would like to borrow something.

➢ Seek out women to talk to while you travel—on trains, in restaurants or cafés, or while shopping. You will learn a lot from local women that will enhance your travels. They are usually as pleased to meet you as you are to meet them.

ROOMMATE CHECKLIST

➤ When you find out who your roommate will be, call her and introduce yourself. This is a good time to tell her a bit about yourself and delicately and honestly to approach the topic of snoring. Ask her, "Do you snore?" Better to find out before the trip and take along earplugs, or find another roommate, than to find out the first sleepless night.

➤ On the first day establish ground rules, including showering times, choosing beds, storage space, and dividing the bathroom counter space. That way there is no misunderstanding.

➤ Describe your preferred "morning mood." I am silent and greatly appreciate quiet or soft conversations; I like to exercise in the morning, so when you wake up I may be gone. This way she won't worry if she wakes up and you aren't there.

➤ Promise to give one another some time alone in the room every day. This should be a minimum of thirty minutes. Set up an agreeable schedule ahead of time, and when it is your turn to give your roommate her time, go for a walk, read, or send email from the lobby or a local café.

Just because you are roommates, you don't have to spend all of your time together. Communicate clearly that you came on the trip to meet a lot of new people.

XV

Boomers on the Go

If I had my life to live over again, I'd try to make more mistakes
the next time. I would relax. I would limber up. I would be stiller
than I have been. I would take more chances. I would take more
trips. I would climb more mountains, swim more rivers,
and watch more sunsets.

—*Nadine Stair, "I'd Pick More Daisies"*

IN MY GRANDMOTHER'S DAY, the only acceptable travel for a
middle-aged or older woman was to visit Aunt Pearl in a nearby
town. Normal women in their sixties, seventies and eighties didn't
hike in New Zealand, bike in New England, join a study tour to
Spain, or travel alone. Bus tours and cruise ships were the pre-
dominant form of "mature" travel. Society has changed. Today, as
Boomers stay more active and mature women become more gutsy,
your imagination is the limit.

An experienced septuagenarian traveler, the late Betty Ann Web-
ster once told me, "I have traveled with my husband and children,
with friends of many countries, with a forty-year-old son, and
enjoyed all those trips. I've often found white hair and advanced

age an advantage. For instance, I am
never hassled by men as younger
women traveling by themselves
sometimes are. On the contrary, I'm
often helped, whether I need it or
not. Young Asians call me 'Aunty.'
I have never encountered violence,
either physical or verbal. Traveling,

> Age is no barrier to your
> dreams and goals.
>
> ♦
>
> —*Helen Thayer, author
> of Polar Dream*

especially alone, involves risk, trust, judgment, and probably luck. But doesn't life itself, wherever you are?"

Grandparents are also spending valuable time with their grandchildren traveling. Travel presents an invaluable opportunity to get to know your grandchildren in unique contexts. Indeed, more and more intergenerational families are taking to the road, the skies, the seas, and the rails . . . and loving it. Everyone is enriched by cross-generational bonding, grandparent mentoring, and different generations learning and exploring together.

No matter how old you are, it's never too late to travel.

TIPS

➤ If you plan to travel with a group, at the time you're doing your research be sure to ask about "single supplements." Several travel companies will not charge you an extra fee if they cannot find you a roommate. (See Resources section for contact information.)

➤ Look for special-interest tours and groups or organize a journey around a special passion.

➤ Ask the tour company for a list of passengers who have gone on the tour you wish to take. Call several of them and ask them what they thought of the trip.

At age sixty, I flew with a friend to Jasper, Alberta, and we rode our bikes to Denver—1,800 miles. We crossed the Continental Divide six times. Before we left, everyone told us not to go, that it wouldn't be safe for two women alone. In five weeks no harm came to us. One of the important things I learned was how material things can become an encumbrance and how little you need to get along. I recommend to anyone, any age, if you have a dream, you mustn't put it off five years. Everybody, please, follow your dreams.

♦

—*Mary Mulligan, Denver, Colorado*

> A medical emergency abroad can be quite frightening. Consider trip insurance that offers emergency evacuation.

> Carry a list of phone numbers and addresses for U.S. embassies and consulates in the region in which you're traveling. You can contact them for emergency services. They can also help you find a reputable local doctor, dentist, or hospital.

As a senior citizen, you should know that Medicare does not cover medical expenses overseas. When you travel, be sure to get a policy that will cover you while you are abroad.

♦

—*Olga Murray, Sausalito, California*

ON THE ROAD WITH THE GRANDKIDS

> Share stories of the "olden days." Relate historic events—the first moon landing, Woodstock, and so forth—to enhance your grandchildren's studies.

> Tell your grandchildren stories about their mom and dad when they were young—this can create a strong link between

---

A delightful side effect of developing a shock of white hair is that other travelers often feel a need to help an older woman. Never mind that I'm on my way to shoot the rapids of a wild New Zealand river or explore an ancient shipwreck with a scuba partner. When I patiently listen to a teenager giving directions to a place from which I've just come, it creates a bond that invites further interaction. I've made friendships, uncovered new places, sampled exotic fare, just because for a moment I traded my need to assert self-assurance for the exhilaration of discovery.

♦

—*Judy Wade, Phoenix, Arizona*

Many grandparents choose to take their grandchildren on organized tours or cruises where there will be other kids, organized children's activities, and some downtime for the adults. See the Resource and Reference section for recommended tour operators, cruises, and dude ranches for "Family Travel."

◆

—MB

past and present. Try the following theme: "Let me tell you a story about when your (mother or father) was bad." Children take special delight in hearing about the behavior of their parents, especially the naughty stuff.

➢ Set rules you are comfortable with, even if they are different from their parents'.

➢ You might need more downtime than those feisty squirts—take the grandkids to a park so they can meet children their own age.

XVI

MOTHER-DAUGHTER TRAVEL

*From grandma and her maternal line, I inherited the urge to keep
moving. For the women in my family, getting away from the
ordinary provides impetus to wander. Travel exemplified freedom.*

—*Vera Marie Badertscher, "Traveling Woman," A Mother's World*

———

MORE AND MORE WOMEN are taking to the road in mother-daughter pairs. And with good reason. If you want to know about the inner life of your mother or daughters, you need almost endless opportunities to talk. The journey you take will be to the center of yourself and your relationship. The memories you will cherish for a lifetime.

I was twenty-six when my mother and I took our first trip together—just the two of us. She left my dad in Ohio and came to visit me. We spent the weekend exploring gold-mining towns in the foothills of the Sierra Nevada mountains. We talked and laughed almost every waking moment. Quite by accident, we

---

———

Laura and I have a wonderful time traveling together, but at times it is a challenge for me to travel "college style." Laura, of course, does not have any trouble adjusting to the luxury hotels to which I've become accustomed. The pleasure of traveling with my daughter is how her openness to new adventures off the beaten path affects me.

♦

—*Lenore Thornton, New York City*

---

came upon a river-rafting group preparing to ride the rapids down the Stanislaus River. Without a moment's hesitation, my mother said, "I've always wanted to do this. Let's see if we can join them!" We spent the afternoon shooting the rapids. And I spent months reflecting upon how little I knew about my responsible, schoolteacher mother.

Few things are more rewarding, so don't hesitate to do it.

TIPS

➢ Offer your mother the priceless gift of your time. Treat her to a night away—just the two of you. Plan an activity that will be very special for both of you: an elegant dinner, a play, a nice hotel, or a river-rafting trip.

➢ If your short excursions together are successful, consider traveling together for longer periods, perhaps even booking an organized tour to someplace you both have always wanted to go.

➢ Begin an annual tradition of taking your mother or daughter, or both, on an overnight adventure. You might choose a date near Mother's Day or her birthday.

Wherever my sister, mom, and I go, we look for thrift shops. We check in the phone book for "thrift stores." My sister will give each of us $20 and we'll go in and shop for each other, and when we go home we wrap up our treasures and present them to each other. Then we hoot and laugh and exchange or trade the items. We have found all sorts of goodies: brand new Stewart Wiseman black alligator shoes for $3.50 or a Coach Bag for $4, a Dunny Burke Purse for $19 and an Armani jacket sample for $15. The best thrift shops we've found are on Main Street, Ventura, California, however, we found a unique store in Sedona with Southwestern clothes. We're looking forward to our next trip to San Francisco to investigate a store that caught our attention: "Out of the Closet."

♦

—*Kathy Musser, Akron, Ohio*

- Be honest up front about how to avoid stepping on one another's toes. If your mom hates the way you drive, hand over the keys. If you're miserable unless you have a window seat, let her know before she books the tickets. Talking openly about your trip in advance will allow you to focus on enjoying your time together.

- Give one another space. Just because you're on a trip together doesn't mean that you have to spend every moment in shared company. Create time in the day for each of you to do your own thing.

- Bring along books and music that you can enjoy together. If you're on a longer trip, you and your mother can each bring a few books and then trade. Discuss your opinions of your shared readings during long rides and over meals.

- If your mother is a widow and you are single, and you usually spend the holidays together, consider exploring a new corner of the world instead of staying home. A friend of mine, a widow in her seventies, and her daughter, in her thirties, spend every Christmas holiday making memories—from tramping around Anasazi ruins in the Southwest to cruising in the Indonesian islands.

- If you can work it out, take your daughter on a short business trip. You can show her what your professional life is like away from home and how you use caution to navigate safely in an unfamiliar city. You can share the places you enjoy, such as museums, parks, cafés, and restaurants.

- One of the most rewarding aspects of taking a mother-daughter trip is the way we travel. We dawdle along the road; we pause to stop and stare; we relax over a pot of tea, watching people, being quiet or talking about the idiosyncrasies of life. Be sure to allow for unstructured time in your itinerary.

- If you are traveling with your mother, ask her about her youth, her teenage years, her romances. Share some of your more private memories with her.

- Take your mom on the trip she fantasizes about. If she's always wanted to see her grandmother's birthplace in Mexico, surprise her with a plane ticket and your companionship.

- I try to take each of my daughters individually on a mother-daughter outing every year. I love these trips. They give me the opportunity to focus on one child at a time and appreciate how she is growing and our relationship is changing. There is no sibling rivalry and she has all of my attention. The sibling left at home, of course, is being spoiled rotten by her dad, who is having special father-daughter time with her. It is healthy for everyone in the family. Don't wait until they're grown.

> The best thing about my travels with my mother is that I am always expecting to show her my world and my experiences, living in another country (Cambodia), but instead we end up creating new experiences and discovering a world of our own.
>
> ◆
>
> —*Laura Thornton,*
> *Vietiane*

Mama's passport photo says it all. The impish grin is brighter than the white curls, the wrinkle of smile deeper than the wrinkles of age. She's happy. She's going somewhere. With me. The mug shot proves I shouldn't have waited so long to invite her. We'd talked about a big trip we'd take "sometime," but I married and got even busier at home and work, and summers and years passed with no adventure together. Then Daddy died. Out of those sad days of winter came a sense of urgency. Time and life were galloping past, and I needed to catch up.

◆

—*Mary Ellen Botter, Prosper, Texas*

XVII
Taking the Kids

It is a wise parent who gives her children roots and wings.
—*Chinese Proverb*

———————

IRONICALLY, IT'S WHEN WE are at home that our lives most easily drift away from the deeper sense of family that we treasure. By that I mean our lives become so dominated by routines, job stresses, and the different demands of each child at each stage, that we can easily lose perspective on what is most important to us.

When traveling, my husband and I converge back into the core of this magical relationship that is family. We depend on each other for guidance, help, and fun. We deal with unforeseen problems and accidental delights, and get to know each other better. We weave a tapestry of common stories to tell over and over. And when we return home from our travels, all is new, and we are closer and more connected.

Time on the road lends itself to long talks, storytelling, games, and reading aloud. Parents whose lives are harried at home get to spend a different kind of time with their children. A family vacation is a time out from day-to-day life when every person has a chance to be heard, to listen, and to participate. A family pulls together to become a self-sufficient team—deciphering maps, interpreting road signs, working through problems, and making decisions. Children have open-ended playtime and interaction. They become better friends as they rely upon each other, even as they squabble more and learn to resolve disputes in a different way than they might at home.

Children learn by actively participating in the greater world around them. When they visit non-English speaking countries, they get to experience what if feels like to be an outsider, a "foreigner." They return home and look at foreigners in their own country with more understanding. Exposure to different cultures and people teaches children tolerance and compassion. And they also learn how to handle difficulties on the road. It is normal to experience delays, for things to go wrong, and to get tired and cranky. Taking cues from you, they can learn patience, how to laugh in the face of adversity and keep going.

Traveling with your children is one of the best investments you can make in the future of your family. Everyone benefits: deepening the commitment of each member to the family, strengthening sibling relationships, savoring moments of expressed love, and creating memories that last a lifetime.

Before we had kids, my husband and I were sure our style of travel wouldn't change; we would just haul our children with us—everywhere. But along with the sleepless nights, diapers, bibs, blankets, and colic came a foreboding premonition that I would never travel again in any way. Although my children didn't exactly stop me, they slowed me down (sometimes for the better). I learned when to take them along and when to go alone.

I am a strong advocate of numerous family vacations each year. Unfortunately, our trips are usually short. But I feel almost any getaway is worth the hassle.

> To protect your children, don't travel with hats, bags, or backpacks that display their names. A stranger could call your child by name, gain his/her confidence more easily, and convince your child you sent the stranger to get them.
>
> ♦
>
> —MB

Let me clarify what I mean by family. I don't just mean the "Ozzie and Harriet" nuclear family of mom, dad, and 2.4 children. Today's family may be any combination of children with a single parent, significant others, friends, or grandparents.

Some of the gutsiest women I know and admire are single moms who travel with their children all the time, almost everywhere. At a book signing in Fairlawn, Ohio, a single mom told me her story of driving to Alaska with her three-year-old daughter and camping for two months. I was humbled by her courage. She was still amazed and empowered by her adventure. Such stories are not unusual. I applaud every mom who has taken her children camping or traveling on her own.

Traveling with children is very different from traveling by yourself, with your spouse, or with a friend. Although you may, as I did, have great trepidation about traveling with your children, you will soon learn that the rewards and memories are worth every inconvenience. My children have opened up new worlds for me. They have given me a different and refreshing perspective on everything we do and see. Together we make more friends and feed off each other's energy and adventurous spirits.

TIPS

➢ Everyone should be involved—from planning the trip and packing to making decisions on the road. As soon as you know where you are going, involve your children: check out books and magazines from your library, mark up a map, discuss what distance you will travel, how long it will take to get there, and what they will do during this time. Let the kids take part in the selection of the toys, games, books, and art materials you take along.

➢ Children learn responsibility when they compose their own packing lists and pack their own bags. It builds confidence and decision-making skills. Show them your lists and discuss how

---

Traveling is your children's best teacher. When they observe how other people live in other places, they not only learn about the wider world but about their world, too. Just don't expect them to express their thanks for the trips you've taken together. Appreciation will only come later in life.

◆

—*Claire Walter, Boulder, Colorado*

you are packing and making plans in advance. They can make sure that their favorite clothes are clean the day before departure. It is a good idea to confirm that they have the essentials.

➤ Plan age-appropriate activities. Each day should include something of interest for everyone. Take into consideration your youngest child's interests and abilities and then work your way through the interests of each family member, including yourself.

➤ Rest and relaxation should be high on your list of activities. Plan quiet time or naps. Picnics are a great way to slow down your pace. Find a park where they can run around and meet other kids while you put your feet up and read some of your book.

Traveling with infants teaches you one lesson: surrender. Give in. Keep your travel plans simple. We eventually learned that the easiest way for us to travel with our young children was to rent a cottage or cabin and stay in one place. We limited our travel time to the journey of getting there and returning. Everyone was happier. Once everyone adjusted to our new environment and began to sleep and eat on a normal schedule again, we relished our free time to play with and savor our children.

—MB

➤ Keep it simple. Underplan your days and move at a leisurely pace so you don't feel rushed. Traveling with children, you won't be able to see or do as much as you would without them. They need extra time to get dressed, go to the bathroom, have snacks, and work off extra energy.

➤ You can simplify your life if you locate and use the restrooms as soon as you arrive at an attraction or museum.

➤ Snacks and filling food are essential. If you feed them, they will be happy. At all times carry drinks and stick-to-your-ribs snacks like apples, bagels, or low-fat granola bars.

- It is helpful to set expectations for a vacation prior to departure. Discuss how things will be different where you are going. Prepare your kids for new kinds of food, entertainment, toilets, languages, long travel days, and periods of "down time." Children are more agreeable if they know what to expect.

- On long trips, children get by with very few clothes or toys and they learn how little they really need to be happy. Encourage them to pack lightly.

- When traveling, children quickly learn that their favorite foods and entertainment are not available everywhere, and that some of their favorite foods may indeed be considered disgusting by others—and vice versa. Most kids

> The grade school years are some of the best years for family travel. It is wonderful to travel with children who are past the toddler stage and yet still pre-teen. They love airports, they love eating, they love treats, they love to learn, they love being with you, and will usually listen to you and they have a sense of wonder about out planet and nature. They're more cooperative than babies and more enthusiastic than many a teenager.

♦

—MB

One thing I love about traveling with my two sons is that I get to see every new place from its highest point. The instant we arrive, they head for the top. I call family trips our "climb-every-crumbling-staircase-to-the-highest-point-in-the-village" itineraries. But of course, depending on locale, we're also used elevators, fire towers, foot paths, chair lifts, cliff-hanging roads. My boys have cheered me on to some of the most spectacular vistas in my life.

♦

—Jo Broyles Yohay, 57, writer.

will try new foods and abandon picky eating habits. They will discover new and simple ways to entertain themselves.

➤ If you are traveling long distances by car with small children, and you want to arrive at your destination with time to spare, rise at 4:30 or 5:00 A.M. and pack your vehicle before everyone else awakes. Pack swimsuits and pajamas in separate bags so they are easily accessible. This way you will not have to break down all your bags to get at one item.

➤ Learn some elements of the language as a family before you travel to a foreign country. Your children will not only benefit from beginning to learn a new language, they will get to use it practically and make friends more easily, even if they know only a few key phrases and words.

➤ If an extended trip is not possible, take your child to a local ethnic market or check out a culture-appropriate video from the library.

➤ History "sticks" when children actually see where it took place. Being in a noteworthy place makes a far stronger impression than most books can. Background material will enhance the experience, however, so check out relevant books from the library before you go.

➤ Stop at tourist information booths or offices. Your children can pick up brochures and create scrapbooks from them. You may also learn about a festival or museum—or cave—you were unaware of (and may discover a family member has an interest you never suspected).

➤ Travel teaches kids to take pleasure from exploring the natural world—watching a

In our family, we have a slogan: "If it is free, we go and see; if you have to pay, we stay away." State parks, national forest campgrounds, and motels in small towns are bargains.

◆

—Doris Scharfenberg,
Farmington Hills,
Michigan

tide pool, collecting pinecones to make forest dolls, rolling down grassy hillsides, seeing an eagle hunt. Try to spend unstructured time outdoors.

➣ Trips are a great way to make geography come alive. Show your children the intended route on the map and explain how long it will take to go from point A to point B. Use city and state maps for shorter excursions. Get a felt-tip pen and draw your route; it will be a wonderful souvenir and memory prompt later, even if it is in tatters.

➣ Kids learn about other cultures by exposure to them: attending a rodeo in Wyoming, observing a tribal powwow in New Mexico, staying in a home in Ireland, visiting a pottery workshop in Mexico, meandering through a market in any developing country, or buying hot, fresh tortillas at a tortilleria in Baja.

➣ For really picky eaters, consider offering the child a coin in the local currency for every new food they try.

➣ Kids need lots of physical activity. Carry action toys— such as a frisbee, inflatable beach ball, or tennis ball— with you at all times for an impromptu sports game.

➣ Buy postcards in the airport or in gift shops. Travel time is great for writing to friends, or grandparents.

> When you arrive at a museum, head for the gift ship. Have your children look through the postcards depicting artwork in the museum's collection and pick out five of their favorites, then have them search for them on your tour of the museum.
>
> ◆
>
> —*Carole Terwilliger Meyers, Oakland, California*

➣ Pack a small magnetic checker or chess board, back-gammon, cards, and dominos for family tournaments. On travel days or during rainy weather you may experience long periods of confinement that wouldn't occur at home.

➤ Remind your child often (both at home and on vacation) of the "buddy system." No one should go anywhere—outhouse, playhouse, beach—without a buddy, whether that is a sibling, parent, or friend.

When the inevitable question arises—what should we do now?—remember that kids love animals (think zoos, aquariums, discovery or natural history museums), parks (play structures, hiking trails and picnic areas) and water (lakes, beaches, pools, water slides) and your attention (read tell stories from when you were a child, play board games such as Yahtzee, checkers, or dominoes). And remember it's O.K. to be bored.

◆

—MB

➤ Travel teaches children how to be flexible as the family encounters delays, cancellations, reservation mix-ups, closed attractions, full restaurants, rude people. They will learn to remain calm and enjoy the adventure if you do.

➤ Memories are made from such brief moments. A trip of only a few short days or weeks in reality will last a lifetime. Children will never forget learning how to make a campfire, bathing under a waterfall, eating mangoes on the beach under a full moon, walking across an airport tarmac, or mimicking unforgettable characters on the road.

➤ Traveling together will change your family. You will discover each other as individuals and appreciate each other's unique characteristics. So keep a record of the trip and the changes you observe in each other. Describe funny situations, conversations, and memorable comments that each person makes in your travel journal.

BABIES & TODDLERS

➤ Proper equipment is essential. Consider the environment to which you are traveling. Strollers are great for cities. Child carries (frontpacks/backpacks) work better on beaches, in rural areas with uneven pavement, and in large crowds

➤ Bring your own carseat for the journey if you are renting a car. Most rental agencies can't guarantee one. The one you bring from hom will also give your child a sense of familiarity.

➤ Arrange for cribs ahead of time. Some hotels have a limited number.

➤ Everyone becomes dehydrated when traveling. Take along a water bottle for each child filled with their favorite drink. Dilute juices and avoid artificially sweetened drinks as they often increase thirst rather than reduce it. Make sure to do a leak check before it goes in their backpacks. Include a large bottle of water for yourself.

➤ When each child is old enough, they should have a backpack that they fill with favorite toys, books, or stuffed animals. Before departure, be sure they have included essential travel items, and that they have left the pet turtle or mouse at home.

➤ Consider using a backpack so that you have your hands free to hold onto your child when you are in crowded airports, amusement parks, or museums.

➤ One joy of traveling with infants is their portability and babies love to be held. They will cooperate and sleep more if you use a chest-style carrier to tote them in.

➤ A small plastic bucket for each child offers younger children on a car trip easy access to a few favorite toys or pocket-sixed books.

➤ Plan to dine early. If the restaurant accepts reservations, call in advance, even for a very early dinner. There may be lots of other families planning to have an early dinner too. If the restaurant doesn't accept reservations, arrive before the peak hours to avoid long waits. Carry quiet toys, crayons, and paper.

➤ Plan the day's activities keeping in mind the baby's normal schedules for feedings, awake, and nap times. They can't keep up with an adult pace. Whenever possible, let them eat and go to bed at their regular meal and bed times.

➤ Parents or adults traveling together should spell each other of child care duties so each person can have time alone. Dad takes one afternoon, mom takes another, and maybe hire a babysitter to have at least one adult night out.

➤ Unscented baby diaper wipes can also serve as hand and face wipes for the whole family, as well as cool off foreheads, wash away blood and dirt from scrapes and scratches, clean up spills, and spiff up sand toys.

FAMILY TRAVEL SAFETY TIPS

➤ In a car, always buckle up your children, no matter how much they protest. A person is four times more likely to be killed and thirteen times more likely to be injured when thrown from a car.

➤ Keep your baby in the car safety seat. Stop if you have to feed or comfort your baby. A 10-pound infant in a three mile per hour crash would be ripped from your arms with a force of 200 pounds.

➤ Safety belts are made for one person. Children should not share them.

➤ Don't use pillows or cushions to boost your child.

➤ Stop for frequent rests, exercising, and toilet breaks.

➤ Children should carry their own identification inside their packs, in purses, or sewn into their clothing.

➤ Kids and ticks go together like peanut butter and jelly. Although most ticks are harmless, Lyme disease, caused by the bite of a rare and tiny tick, is a serious concern for every parent. Be prepared when hiking in unfamiliar areas. Prevention is not always easy. It is recommended that you and your kids wear long sleeves and long pants in the woods and grassy areas. Take a shower after being outside and check yourself and your child carefully.

➤ If you do find a tick, remove it gently but firmly with tweezers. Take your time. If you pull too hard or twist, you may leave the head embedded in the body. Wipe the skin with antiseptic. Keep the tick. Put it in a jar to show medical authorities later if necessary. Watch for any skin reaction or any unusual symptoms and contact a physician immediately if they occur.

➤ On family vacations it seems that everyone gets a large dose of sunshine, but sunburn for a child is serious. Pack lots of sunscreen (SPF fifteen or greater); use it thirty minutes before going into the sun and reapply every two hours, even if the product is touted as waterproof. Cloudy days are just as dangerous as sunny days.

➤ Pack a broad-brimmed hat or bonnet to protect your child's face, ears, and scalp. Keep babies out of the sun entirely.

➤ Bees love sweets, watermelon, and burgers. So do kids. What do you do when the two meet? Remove the stinger with a horizontal scraping motion, using your fingernail or something flat like a driver's license. Don't squeeze or pull the stinger or you'll release more venom. Clean the site with soap and water and apply ice compresses. Make a paste of unseasoned meat tenderizer or baking soda (if you happen to have some with you) and water and apply to the area. This will neutralize the remaining venom.

FIRST AID KIT

➤ When traveling with kids your first-aid kit should include tweezers (with pointed tips), bandages, gauze, fancy Band-aids, antibacterial soap, adhesive tape, first aid/antibacterial cream or ointment, child-and-adult-strength ibuprofen or aspirin, syrup of ipecac (for poison), thermometer, age-appropriate motion sickness medication, sunscreen, and anti-histamine for allergic reactions. A bottle of unseasoned meat tenderizer is handy for bee or wasp stings. Zip-lock bags make quick ice packs with a hand towel for a cover.

XVIII
TRAVEL WITH TEENS

Traveling with teenagers can be tough.
—*Marybeth Bond*

———

ATTITUDE WITH AN A, sullen silence and mono-syllabic conversations are only half the fun of traveling with teens. Add to this the pungent aroma of smelly socks (teenage boys), or being locked out of the bathroom for hours (teenage girls) and you might wonder if family travel is such a good idea during this chaotic/self-absorbed adolescent stage.

Is it worth all the patience required and money it costs to travel with teens? Yes. Why? Travel can expand and renew communication within the family and provide a stimulating way to spend time together as your teens approach the age when they will leave the nest. And a lot of teens are fun companions and have loads of energy for activities. But how do you travel so everyone enjoys it and you don't come home with a head of gray hair and an unhappy/belligerent kid?

When considering a trip with teens, there are three basic principles to keep in mind: involve them, burn calories, and negotiate.

Involve your teens in the travel planning process from the very beginning. If you present several vacation ideas and they help make the decision and pitch in with the planning, then they share responsibility for the success of the trip. Many of them are savvy enough to do detailed research on the Internet where there is a plethora of travel-related information.

The library and bookstores are filled with guides, magazines, videos, brochures, foreign and language tapes that will make your kids feel more familiar with the place they are traveling. While researching a vacation, they'll learn geography, how to read maps and guidebooks, how to make a budget (very important), and what resources are available and where.

Consider trips that appeal to their interests—do they want to learn how to surf, sail, horseback ride, learn about the Navajo Nation, dig for artifacts, visit the Rock'n'Roll Hall of Fame or a Baseball Spring Training Camp in Arizona.

You can tailor your vacation to your teens interests or to who your teen is becoming. For example, if your teen is interested in marine life, get certified together and go on a scuba diving trip. Make it a surprise graduation present from middle or high school. Kids can get certified starting at twelve-years-old.

Teens need to burn calories! Boisterous, hormone-driven kids thrive on daily physical activity. Sports-oriented vacations channel your teens' abundant energy, and provide opportunities to acquire outdoor skills, make new friends and build self-confidence. Amazing things happen on active vacations—mom learns to belay while the kids learn to rappel, or the whole family bikes together, until the big hill leading to the pass, and then the kids will leave the "old people" in the dust . . . unless you and your spouse are in fantastic shape. Keeping up with the kids can be the incentive for going to the gym before a family vacation.

On any trip, keep in mind that a tired teenager is a kid that won't get in trouble and you won't have fret about their whereabouts as much. Better to have them pooped out in the tent, cabin or hotel room at night than out looking for excitement. Teens are also more civil after exercise.

Negotiate—trade activities and interests. For example, "Mom really wants to view the Matisse exhibit so how about in exchange we'll take you to a pizza place tonight." or: "We'll sight see in the morning and shop for you in the afternoon."

Give them slack. At times let them stay up really late to watch a movie or read, then sleep until noon. Go out and do some sightseeing without them, if you trust the alone. Time apart from each other makes the time together less stressful. Don't be the trip dictator. Let them make restaurant and activity choices too.

Family camps or organized family trips, with specially-designed teen programs, are good choices because their activities are supervised and contained within safe boundaries. Numerous family camps offer classes from whitewater kayaking, rock climbing or the basics of sailing, to windsurfing, horseback riding and mountain biking.

When our kids were teens we joined a multi-sport family trip to the San Juan Islands in Washington. They met other teens and formed their own group for biking, kayaking, hiking and after-dinner get-togethers. We, their parents, became good friends and enjoyed the activities at our own pace.

THEME PARKS

➢ When you arrive at theme parks, museums, and other crowded tourist attractions, select a central meeting place just in case you get separated from your kids. Counsel them on how to identify and approach an employee to ask for help if they think they are lost. If they need to locate you in a crowd, advise them to call you by your first names. There will be lots of other mommies and daddies.

➢ Have your children memorize the name of your hotel. Give them a hotel business card to keep in their pocket.

➢ Encourage your kids to wear bright-colored tops so they are more visible in a crowd.

XIX
VOLUNTEER TRAVEL

Never doubt that a small group of thoughtful, committed citizens
can change the world. Indeed, it is the only thing that ever has.
—*Margaret Mead*

SOMETIMES UNSTRUCTURED, FREE-WHEELING TRAVEL
is as good as it gets—a delicious break from the regimens of our
busy, over-planned lives. Other times nothing surpasses the rewards
of planting yourself in one place and digging in. For travel with a
meaningful twist, consider volunteering or joining theme-oriented
journeys.

If you're craving a deeper connection to the places you're visiting, ready to throw yourself into a project, and excited to meet and work with people from all over the world, I highly recommend volunteering during your travels. Volunteering on the road can require as minimal a commitment as a day or as extensive a commitment as a couple of years. It all depends on what you want to do and the flexibility of your plans. Yet, regardless of the length or nature of your volunteer stint, it will likely be one of the most rewarding parts

> Teaching in Japan gave me a depth of knowledge and insight into the culture that I would not otherwise have gained, even through years of study. While not always easy, nothing else I've done has been nearly as worthwhile or rewarding. I learned at least as much as I taught, and I left with some of the most vivid memories and deepest friendships of my life.
>
> ♦
>
> —*Tara Weaver, Seattle, Washington*

of your trip. Volunteering feeds the soul. It immerses you more deeply than you could imagine and will leave its imprint long after the project ends.

Many international organizations offer an array of volunteer and work-abroad options as far-ranging as an archaeological dig in Israel, trail maintenance in Yellowstone National Park, school-building in Nicaragua, caring for the dying at Mother Teresa's hospice in Calcutta, museum restoration in England, and teaching English in Tunisia. Volunteer possibilities are innumerable—what matters is finding the right match for you.

TIPS

➤ Determine your interests, needs, and reasons for volunteering. The clearer you are about what you want, the more likely you'll choose your project well, and the less likely you'll feel disappointed or frustrated by your experience.

➤ Take into account your abilities and limitations—emotional, physical, intellectual, and financial. For instance, do you have a bad back? If so, a project involving hard manual labor and lots of bending—such as building a house—might not be for you. Likewise, if you're highly skilled at working with people, consider putting that ability to use in your volunteer work.

➤ Research the organizations you come across and try to avoid committing to the first opportunity that pops up. You want to know as much as possible about the organization with which you work and feel confident about what you're getting yourself into.

➤ Talk to alumni of whatever organization/project you're considering. Some of the most honest and accurate evaluations of a program come from those who have gone before you, who have already invested their time, energy, and money. Their experience and wisdom is often invaluable.

- Find out how long the organization has been around. Is its work well respected? Will you feel good about having an affiliation with this organization?

- How much money are you willing or able to spend? The financial costs of volunteer projects vary considerably. Some volunteer opportunities are free, whereas others cost more than a package tour. Don't forget to take into account the cost of getting to the work location.

- How do you feel about groups? Most volunteer projects involve working closely with a group of strangers. (Of course they won't be strangers for long.) Working together can be one of the most rewarding ways to get to know people, including those from different countries and backgrounds, but also one of the most challenging. As with all travel, it helps to be flexible, open, and up for the adventure.

- Find out how much time you'll have to yourself. Will you have days off? An hour of solitary time each day? Or will most of your time be determined by the structure of the program? How many hours per day are you expected to work? Is there any flexibility?

> When you volunteer in a foreign country you are welcomed into the homes and hearts of local people.
>
> ♦
>
> —MB

- Are you traveling with your family? Ask if kids can participate. If not, is there something else for them to do in the area?

- Don't expect things to operate exactly as they do back home. While the differences may be charming to the short-term visitor or tourist, those volunteering or working abroad for long stints may get frustrated when systems do not function in familiar ways. Be prepared and, when it happens, relax. This is an opportunity to learn how things work locally and how to approach the situation next time around.

> Realize that it may not be possible to accomplish as much as you initially planned—not that you shouldn't try. Language, cultural differences, tradition, and pace of life may prove challenging obstacles to your original objectives. If this happens, don't despair. Reevaluate your goals and focus on what is achievable, given the specifics of the situation. There is no failure in altering your plans once you've learned what is truly possible and worth pursuing.

> While travelers often exist in a constant state of discovery, when you settle into a place for longer stretches it is possible to slip into a daily pattern. Don't lose sight of the incredible opportunity you have to explore your host culture. Make a list of things you want to accomplish in your time overseas, whether it's studying traditional arts or languages, visiting specific places, or experiencing special events or festivals. By organizing your time and setting goals, you can make sure your time is well spent—it will be over before you know it.

> Check out the International Volunteer Programs Association (IVPA) at www.volunteerinternational.org. IVPA is an alliance of nonprofit organizations offering a great range of international volunteer and internship opportunities. For other reputable organizations doing good work around the world, turn to the Resources section.

THEME-ORIENTED TRAVEL

> Theme-oriented travel presents another good way to deepen and focus your experiences on the road. It allows you to connect travel to your passions or nurture a fledgling interest.

> Do you love to cook? Are you fascinated by Thailand? Why not attend a cooking school in Bangkok? Is the Maine coast your favorite place to vacation, and you've just picked up photography? The seaside village of Rockport hosts one of the most extensive photography programs in the country. Are you dying to learn Spanish, as well as tromp around for a

few months with a backpack? Why not enroll in a language-immersion school in Quito, Ecuador? You'll be surprised by how quickly you learn the language in such an intensive context, and then you can explore South America with new communication skills.

➢ Consider what type of vacation you want when selecting your tour, trek, language program, holistic center, or painting workshop. Do you want something intensive or relaxed? Something solitary or with a group? Would you rather spend a weekend away or a month? As always, the clearer you are about your wants and needs, the wiser your choices will be.

➢ Create your own special itinerary. You don't necessarily need a tour, program, or school to explore your interests while traveling. Do a little research about the place you're going. Find out about the museums, wildlife, handicrafts or whatever it is that makes your heart soar, and build a trip around your passion.

XX
PACKING

On a long journey even a straw weighs heavy.
—*Spanish proverb*

———

BEFORE EVERY TRIP I agonize about what to pack. Should I use my roll-aboard, a sturdy duffel bag, or a big suitcase? Which shoes, coats, clothing should I take?

To reduce this stress I begin to tuck items into my bag days before departure. For a short trip, I might pack one or two days in advance. For an adventure trip, such as trekking in the Himalayas, I begin checking my gear (hiking boots, fanny pack, warm coats, flashlights, etc.) weeks before.

Recently I packed in two days for a two-week trip—camping in the Sahara Desert, exploring Morocco's Atlas Mountains, Roman ruins, and imperial cities. How? The adventure travel company who operated the trip sent me a comprehensive packing list. All my gear fit into one duffel bag, and, surprisingly, I didn't have to buy any new clothes or equipment. And keep the packing list for next time.

I like lists. They keep me organized. I keep several versions in my luggage and highlight in bright yellow the items I continually forget, such as dental floss, belts, and fresh batteries for flashlights. My goal is to pack so efficiently that when I unpack after a trip I discover I have worn or used every item in my bag.

TIPS

➤ When in doubt, leave it out—a good packing motto to help remind you to pack lightly.

- ➤ Pack doubles of anything you really can't live without, like your contact lenses, prescription sunglasses, a copy of your passport, driver's license, or credit card. I even pack two tubes of lip balm and stuff my empty shoes with feminine hygiene supplies.

- ➤ Keep all your luggage organized. Bring zip-lock bags with you. One week into your trip, you'll wish you had brought more. They keep freshly washed but not-quite-dry underwear separated from dry clothes, pills and vitamins separate from snacks. These see-through bags, available in all sizes make it easy to find everything from tampons to batteries to flashlights.

- ➤ Pack comfy walking shoes. Your shoes must be well worn in before you leave on the trip. Pack extra socks that dry quickly and wick the moisture away from your feet. Bring moleskin in case you develop blisters. Also consider bringing talcum powder to sprinkle in your shoes if you will be walking a lot. This prevents rashes and sweaty feet in hot climates. Wear your bulkiest, heaviest pair of shoes or hiking boots on the plane.

- ➤ Bring one quick-drying travel outfit. Cotton, wool, and linen clothing is impractical, heavy, and outdated for your travel wardrobe.

- ➤ New travelwear for women combines practical design with performance fabric. Quick-drying fabrics enable on-the-road wash and wear, while others even remove moisture from your body. This type of fabric is designed for wear on sea-kayaking trips, alpine treks, rafting adventures, and any other activity where

High-quality binoculars are a "must" on wildlife/nature trips, such as those to Alaska and Africa. Each person should have his/her own pair. Affix a label on the binoculars, as well as on the case, so if they're misplaced, they can easily be returned to you.

♦

—*MB*

you may get wet but must stay dry and warm. Dress in layers. Shop from a specialized travel catalog or store.

➤ Invest in an all-weather travel coat. Although your choice will depend upon the climate of your destination and your adventure activities, a rainproof all-weather coat is essential. It should be light, have many pockets, and feature a hood.

I never travel without a sarong. Sometimes it can be a skirt, a dress, a beach cover-up, a belt, a carry-all, a bathrobe, or a tablecloth. It is so versatile.

◆

—Christine Wilson,
Portland, Oregon

➤ Wear layers of clothing if you are going to a place where the climate changes dramatically from day to night or if you plan lots of outdoor activities.

➤ Always pack your bathing suit. You never know when you'll have an opportunity to swim or hop in a hot tub, and there is no better tension reliever.

➤ Shop for good luggage. Try a roll-aboard that will fit under the seat or in the overhead. If a roll-aboard isn't for you, try a sturdy duffel bag with built-in compartments. Shop for these in a store specializing in travel luggage.

➤ When buying travel gear, consider the bag's durability—how much abuse can it take? Look for beefy zippers and finished seams. For the sake of your shoulders, arms, and hands, look for comfy handles and straps.

AVOID DENTAL DISASTERS

➤ Prior to your departure, see your dentist and ask him/her to look for loose fillings or unstable caps. A broken tooth, cap or filling can cause extreme sensitivity or a toothache. Pack a small, inexpensive "Tooth Repair Kit" containing temporary filling material. It is available at most drug stores.

WHAT TO PACK IN YOUR CARRY ON BAG

➤ Carry all your medications with you on the plane, in case your checked luggage gets lost or delayed.

➤ My list of items to take on the plane includes reading materials, earplugs, eye shields, neck pillow, socks, a sweater, several nutritious snacks (granola bar, dried fruit), Chap?stick, toothbrush and toothpaste, extra glasses.

➤ Conquer cold feet. The temperature on airplanes can vary from tropical heat to arctic chill during a flight and you can't count on finding an airline blanket when you need it. Dress in layers, bring a sweater, and pack slipper-socks in your carry-on bag.

➤ The air circulated in airplane cabins is extremely dry. When traveling by plane, carry lip balm and moisturizer to prevent chapped lips and skin.

➤ Inexpensive silicon earplugs reduce the noise on airplanes to help you concentrate on work or reading a good novel. They also regulate the flow of air into your ears and allow you to adapt better to pressure changes. Available at drugstores or airport shops, silicon earplugs (not foam) work the best.

➤ I take unread magazines and newspapers. As I read them, I discard them or give them to other Americans, who always seem to appreciate my cast-off reading material.

➤ Synthetic material (panty hose) will melt in high heat. Recent tests have shown that when women slide down an airplane's emergency escape ramp, the friction and heat generated from the slide melted their nylon stockings to their legs. Chances are you'll never have to exit a plane this way, but just in case, don't wear pantyhose when you fly.

➤ Identify your bags. More and more people are traveling with black roll-aboard suitcases. Twice someone has mistakenly grabbed my roll-aboard off the baggage-claim carousel. To avoid problems, identify your luggage with something colorful, such as yellow or red ID tags, tie a ribbon around the handle, or wrap a colorful strap around the suitcase.

➤ Provide minimal information on baggage identification tags. I list only my first initial, last name, and geographic area. If my bags are lost, airline personnel can locate me through the computer. The information I have provided is too vague for anyone to find my residence, phone number, profession, or place of employment.

➤ Identification tags are often torn off during baggage handling. Be sure to have full identification inside your luggage.

THE BASICS

➤ Money. Consider buying a money belt or pouch and wear your valuables close to your heart (or torso). Keep credit and debit cards, passport, and large bills in it. Don't forget to take about twenty one-dollar bills for tips.

➤ Pack a first-aid kit of pills, bandages, Imodium, Pepto Bismol, Alka Seltzer tablets, tampons, antibacterial gel, sunscreen, lip balm, and mosquito repellent. Another must is an all-purpose antibiotic, such as Ciproflaxacin, which can be used for serious traveler's diarrhea, upper respiratory problems, and more. A prescription is necessary, so consult with your doctor.

➤ Emergen-C or Airborne—I won't leave home without them because they boost my immune system.

➤ Bring a small bottle of anti-bacterial gel. Then you can always wash your hands before meals and after pit stops.

➤ Pack a small flashlight and leave it on your bedside table. If you awake during the night you won't have to fumble for the light switch. If you have a roommate you won't wake her/him if you use your flashlight to go to the bathroom and you can read in bed if your roommate wants to go to sleep before you.

DUCT TAPE TO THE RESCUE

➤ Shampoo—from hair to hosiery. If you're staying in relatively nice hotels, don't bother to pack washing detergent. The shampoo provided by your hotel can be used to wash out underwear or hosiery.

➤ If you're traveling on a budget and your hotels are unlikely to provide shampoo, pack a Zip-lock bag full of detergent for washing your clothes.

Wrap a foot of duct tape around an unsharpened pencil and tuck it in your luggage. Duct tape comes to the rescue is a strap on a sandal snags, a purse handle or backpack strap breaks, or luggage gets ripped.

◆

—MB

➤ Extra batteries are essential for your cameras. If, by accident, you leave the shutter open or flash on overnight, your battery will be dead in the morning. You may not find the size and brand of battery you need easily.

The first things into my suitcase are always the bandannas—at least a half-dozen per trip, in a variety of bright colors. Nothing so light, so easy to pack, has ever played so many roles, saved so many days. The simple cotton squares serve as headbands when hiking; cooling, damp neckerchiefs when worn wet in a steamy jungle; fast-drying washcloths in all those hotels and hostels that don't provide them; or washcloths in camp that can be quick-dipped in a stream and quick-dried, draped over a branch or bush. They are often the only end-of-the-day solution to "hat head" or wilted beach hair, a plague I am prone to even in the desert. Thus, my bandannas go wherever my passport goes. And, invariably, I give the lavenders and yellows and tie-dyes away along the way, coming home even lighter than I left.

◆

—Paula McDonald, Baja California, Mexico

> Pack an extra nylon duffel inside your luggage to store items in a hotel in the event you travel to other cities and want to leave a bag behind. It is also useful as an extra piece of luggage to carry home purchases.

> Take along photos of your home, pets, and family as well as colorful postcards of your hometown. Postcards are easy gifts, and personal photos help you share your world. A puppet or colored pens and pencils will win you friends in developing countries.

HOW TO PACK FOR A CRUISE

> It's easy to pack for a cruise. Resort wear is perfect for daytime activities. Dinner attire, (cocktail dresses or tailored slacks and tops) are for special cocktail evenings and the "Meet the Captain Dinner." I use scarves, jewelry and Pashmina shawls to dress up my little black cocktail dress and simple outfits.

> Linen clothing is elegant and stylish but wrinkles easily when you sit for long periods of time or when it's packed. I prefer knits and cotton blends and to avoid wrinkling.

> I try to buy birthday, anniversary, graduation, mother and father's day gifts in advance and when I'm traveling I often see original gift ideas. A list of friends and family for whom I will need a present in the next six months keeps me focused on buying for others, as well as myself.

> To help me decide who should get the gift, I bring along my shopping list with clothing sizes and birthday dates to help me.

> One of the most important items I pack on wildlife or nature cruises is a high-quality pair of binoculars. Nothing is more frustrating than trying to share binoculars when you are watching a glacier calve or a bear forage on the shore, so each person in your group should have his/her own pair. Make

sure to label your binoculars and case with your name so they can be easily returned if misplaced.

➤ In my experience, it can be hard to find a laundry or laundry service at your hotel or on a cruise that doesn't take 24 to 48 hours, so I sometimes need to wash small items in the sink. I use my shampoo to wash them and the added benefit is the lovely, clean fragrance.

XXI

Stories from the Life of a Gutsy Traveler

THE GUTSY TRAVELER'S LIFE

Akron, Ohio. Age 8.

Every evening when Dad came home from work, he would put his extra change in a bean jar in the kitchen. The money was carefully counted and saved for a splurge on our annual camping vacation. If there was enough money, we'd go out to dinner in a sit-down restaurant or buy hot fudge sundaes. All year long my parents saved and planned for a major family vacation. The day school ended, we would pack up the trailer, stop the mail, unplug the electrical appliances, and cram four kids and two adults into the station wagon. We camped in state and national parks across America from Wisconsin to Florida and Virginia to California.

> I learned how to save money, be frugal, and splurge.

Jackson Hole, Wyoming. Age 17.

During a family trip through the mountainous West, I envied the college students working in lodges and resorts. They were having a blast. My parents always told me to "dream big" and urged me to look for a job for the next summer in a national park. At Jackson Lake Lodge, I wandered into the Human Resource Office and asked for a job interview for employment the following summer. I got lucky. I was not offered a glamorous job as a waitress or receptionist, but as a maid. I talked a girlfriend into joining me, but at the last minute she decided to stay in Akron with her boyfriend. Faced with the dilemma of canceling my dream, or going alone, I chose to go solo. Two days after high school graduation, I left my boyfriend, boarded the airplane by myself and flew to Wyoming to change beds and clean toilets.

A month into the summer, I broke a finger horse-back riding and was promoted to "toast girl" in the kitchen. After a week of buttering toast I was promoted to dining room waitress, a job I loved. Serving rainbow trout or prime rib in the Jackson Lake Lodge restaurant I met well-traveled American and international guests.

For two summers I worked at the lodge, dated cowboys, the pastry chef, and park rangers, and climbed the Grand Teton and made life-long friends from New York and California. Patty, a recent college graduate, regaled me with stories of her year studying and traveling abroad. My experiences and new friends expanded my vision of myself, what my life could be.

> ➤ I realized I could "go alone" and would need to, if I wanted to fulfill my dreams.

Miami University in Oxford, Ohio. Age 19.

During my freshman year in college I began dreaming of leaving Ohio to study in Europe. My family was not in a position to pay for such an adventure, so I had to look elsewhere for financial support. A kind professor helped me apply for an alumni scholarship. The generosity of a university alumni, who loved to travel herself, gave me the opportunity to spend a year in Luxembourg, live with a local family, study, and travel. From London to St. Petersburg, and Crete to Paris, my world expanded as I fell in love with Europe.

> ➤ I learned how much I didn't know about the world and myself.

San Francisco, California. Age 25–29.

After living in Paris for four years after college, I settled in San Francisco and began a career. I was 25 and felt I had to prove myself in corporate America. I needed to succeed and above all, I needed to make money to prove my worth to my colleagues and myself. For four years I worked in high tech, for Xerox, then Honeywell.

By my late twenties I had a nice life, nice things and plenty of money. I was living a conventional life doing what I thought I was supposed to do, conforming to the norm, following the crowd. But I was bored and dissatisfied. I had been too eager to accept what other people told me I should be. But who was I really and what did I want from my future? Did I have the courage to move forward and try other possibilities?

I knew I had to gain some perspective on my life. But what? And how? Then I remembered my childhood dream of traveling around the world, a seed planted by piles of National Geographic magazines in my parents' attic in Ohio. And I dared to dream and dream big. As I scribbled down a wish list of places to explore, I felt energized, empowered, and excited about the life that could be mine. When I made the big decision there was an almost instantaneous change in my energy and mental attitude.

At age 29 I quit my job at Honeywell, put my car, clothing and career in storage and bought a one-way ticket to Bangkok. I took a sleeping pill on the flight over the Pacific because I was terrified of traveling alone. The truth be told, I had never eaten in a restaurant or gone to a movie by myself.

While some thought (and told me) I was nuts, I traveled "single and solo" for two years around the world. It was during my travels that I discovered the "gutsy woman" inside of me. I had the time of my life, and gained valuable insight into myself.

> I learned that money doesn't necessarily bring fulfillment or happiness. I stepped out of my comfort zone into the unknown, and discovered myself.

Asia and Africa. Age 29–30

During my two years traveling across the world, I hiked, biked, dived, danced, snow-shoed, skied, climbed, coptered, trekked and traipsed my way through more than 70 countries. I experienced the unknown on my own terms, across the Himalayas on foot and the Sahara Desert by camel. I dove in the Maldive Islands and climbed to the summit of Mt. Kilimanjaro. I even met my future husband, an American trekker, in Kathmandu.

Travels in Life and Abroad. Age 30s–40s.

Gary, the wonderful man I met in Kathmandu, reappeared in my life soon after my return to the U.S. We were married and had two daughters. We traveled extensively with them, from the Grand Canyon to the Olduvai Gorge in Tanzania. The girls and I traveled alone when he could not accompany us. We lived with a family and studied Spanish in Mexico, rode packhorses and camped with a Navajo grandmother on tribal lands in Arizona, played soccer with their pen pals in Tanzania before a safari, and hiked through the rice terraces of Bali to attend a local wedding.

We escaped the Thailand tsunami during our holiday vacation, but returned home with survivor's guilt. Now when I return to Thailand I am treated like a local when they discover I was with them during the tsunami.

> ➤ I realized the fragility of life and the resiliency of the human spirit.

Biking Across America. Age 50+

When my 22-year-old daughter asked me to join her in the great adventure of riding our bicycles across the country, I jumped at the chance to spend two months with her and to have another huge adventure.

In case you have the impression that I'm a super athlete or adrenaline junkie, I should let you know that I didn't have the experience or qualifications for this undertaking.

For reasons that made perfect sense to us, but not to my husband or most of my friends, we planned to bike across the country, camping, preparing our own meals, charting our own course, unassisted by a professional support van.

Logistical challenges and haunting doubts were our only roadblocks. How would we finance it? Could we get in shape to ride

3,000+ miles? Was I too old? How could we avoid joining a group? Should we buy maps and go by ourselves? Should we ask someone to drive a camper for us? My daughter JC threw down the gauntlet: "Mom, I know you'll find a way."

Two months later, we partnered with a major corporate sponsor and invited JC's best friend to drive the Recreational Vehicle (RV) that would become our home. We contacted the National Osteoporosis Foundation and offered to dedicate our ride to their cause. Why? I am afflicted with osteoporosis, as are my sisters and mother. So we launched a website and blog asking for donations of a "dollar for each mile" we biked. Our goal was to ride across the country and increase awareness of women's bone health. We accomplished the ride; we remained friends; no one was hurt; and perhaps our greatest achievement was raising $52,000 for a worthwhile cause.

Pedaling miles and miles every day I felt more alive and more alert than before. I felt eager with anticipation. I look around with fresh eyes and embraced the world as I slowly pedaled through it, appreciating the fragrance of freshly mowed grass or the taste of dark chocolate washed down with cold water.

On every climb, I recited little mantras in my head, coaching myself to pedal and forget my body. *"Om mani padme om,"* I chanted over and over again, until my body, breath, and everything around me dissolved. And then, to my astonishment, I was at the summit.

Biking was not the only part of my mission. I felt it was important to share the adventure with others who might now be in a position to have an adventure of their own, but could enjoy it vicariously through our blogs and updates.

Some days the most exhausting hours were late at night when I lay on my bed, aching from my waist down, craving solitude, peace and sleep. I forced myself to put aside my negativity, pick up my computer, put things in perspective, and find something positive or insightful to write in our blog. I could hear my mother's voice, "Who ever said it would be easy? Quit your whining and deal with it."

➤ I learned that great satisfaction comes by giving back.

My travel stories that follow describe my hopes and dreams and what became of them. I reflect upon places, adventures and people who have changed my life and made it meaningful.

Whether you read one or all the stories, I hope I can pass on a few of the lessons I learned during my journeys—about life, myself, and what it takes to make a dream come true.

TRAVELING SOLO AROUND THE WORLD

It builds character, and furnishes the palace of memory.

———

By the time I was twenty-nine years old, I had two degrees, a great job in the high tech world, and was living in the beautiful hills of Marin County just across the Golden Gate Bridge from San Francisco. For my age, I had achieved everything our society tells us we should to want.

But I was unhappy. So I did something dramatic, scary and gutsy and it led me on an unorthodox path to fulfillment.

I gave up my job and with it the career that I had worked so hard to build. I was burnt out from years of hard work in sales and marketing for Xerox and Honeywell. I did not like the hard-driving, hard-shelled woman I had become or the life I had made for myself.

I packed up my house, put all my belongings, including my car, into storage and took off for a year-long sojourn through Asia, and then a second year traveling through Africa and Europe.

I traveled alone into remote corners of the world and my life was woven in and out of the lives of villagers, tribesmen, explorers, climbers and craftsmen. Unconventional methods of travel—from camels and elephants to back waterway barges and my own two feet—led my pilgrimage. One important and unexpected aspect of my travels was a growing involvement with eastern spirituality. A lifelong Presbyterian, I wound up spending time in an Indian ashram studying meditation under a famous holy teacher.

When I began my journey, I found it very hard to say goodbye to my dearest friends and relatives, not to mention a promising career and a comfortable life. Returning was equally difficult. I had to bid the experience of travel itself farewell, to accept the limits of the trip, and to reorient myself toward a "normal" nine to five work life. I made a tremendous life change, reinventing myself, starting over in a new profession and with a new self-image.

My experience of going solo around the world is more than an adventure story. It is the inner journey of a successful contemporary career woman who confronts the flaws in the American dream and risks her identity, her financial future and sometimes her life to undergo a metamorphosis that enables her to start off in a new direction upon her return.

When I returned, I changed directions; I assumed responsibility for myself and started over again. Mine is the story of one young woman's rite of passage.

Travel is, or can be, as much an inward as an outward experience, and mine proved to involve an important inner dimension. Cut off from all of my support systems, I was tested in some rather wild situations. I learned a great deal about myself – how to be alone, how to live according to an inner-determined course, how to stay in touch with the feminine qualities within me, how to expand my capacity to give and receive and how necessary it is to laugh at myself.

Since my stories and articles about my solo travels have been published worldwide I have been flooded with letters and inquiries from women and men alike. I have been invited to lecture and have appeared on radio and television, including the Oprah Winfrey Show.

Two questions everyone asked me about my travel alone were:

"Did you get the runs?" and, "Did you find God?"

Yes, of course; and, It depends on what you mean by that.

Two things I did find for certain: myself and the man who would later become my husband.

ROMANCE IN KATHMANDU

A moment is all it takes.

━━━━

I was sitting on a low sofa in the lobby of the Kathmandu Guest House, having just returned from the trails of Annapurna. I hadn't washed my hair in ten days; the last thing on my mind was romance.

Then, I saw his legs: long, lean and muscular. I learned that he was leaving the next morning for a month's trek to Mt. Everest. Our paths crossed for one moment. Long enough to light a spark.

I continued my travels for another year. And, within days of my return to San Francisco, we met again at a mutual friend's party.

Romance, then marriage, then children. It was meant to be.

PEDALING THROUGH THE EMERALD ISLE

She discovers that the Emerald Isle has a song in its heart,
and chivalry at its core.

———————

If life seems richer, greener, and more melodic in Ireland, that's because there is simply more clear air, clean water, verdant countryside, and heart-lifting music in everyday life.

For ten entrancing days, I cycled the quiet back roads of the Ring of Kerry and the Dingle Peninsula in southwest Ireland. By day, I wheeled down corkscrew lanes aflame with red fuchsia and yellow gorse, through frog-green hills crisscrossed with ancient stone walls, dotted with medieval ruins, and grazed by baaing sheep. By night, I basked in the musical revelry of a local pub or the warmth of farmhouse hospitality.

I quickly discovered that, for a relatively small island (the size of Maine), Ireland offers an extraordinary variety of scenery and a network of intertwining trails and bike-perfect country lanes. Indeed, Ireland is a hiker's and cyclist's paradise.

Spinning through pastures of myriad shades of green, past high hedges, and rushing rivers, I felt the earth roll under my pedals, smelled the peat bricks burning, and tasted the salty air of the coast, where the ocean foamed onto rocky shores. Along the Dingle Peninsula I stopped often to rest on a towering cliff above the treacherous coastline and watch 3,000 miles of Atlantic surge towards the beach.

This was my first trip to Ireland and I traveled alone. Although I would have enjoyed biking with a buddy or significant other, no one had the same vacation time, so I took off solo—to a country reputed to be safe and hospitable. The glossy photos in the tour brochures I consulted showed smiling guests at sumptuous feasts, experienced guides, a support vehicle for cyclists, and luxurious accommodations in castles and manor houses. But an organized bike trip didn't fit my slim budget, so I spent my nights in cozy cottages, farmhouses, and small B & Bs, where the matron of the house would tuck a hot water bottle in the toe of my bed while I went out for dinner.

And while bicycle tour companies provide their guests with twenty-one-speed hybrid touring models, my rented vehicle was a one-speed, heavy black bike with a wire basket in front, resembling the bicycle Dorothy's wicked neighbor rode in *The Wizard of Oz*. I squeezed my backpack into the basket and headed for the open road.

For me, the allure of exploring rural Ireland by bicycle was the slow pace and the up-close contact with the land and the people. I could pedal along the most scenic routes, stop often, breathe the fragrant air, gaze out upon the verdant landscape, and remember every heart-pounding hill that passed under my wheels. My feelings of exhilaration came in a smug, distinctly self-satisfied way, in the burn I felt just before I hauled myself by pedal power to the top of yet another hill. Or after a long day in the saddle, knowing my muscles were harder. Or in the slight tingle in my calf muscles that reminded me I just had the most inspiring day's ride ever.

Starting in popular Killarney, I rode around the Ring of Kerry, along the perimeter of the Iveragh Peninsula, and then along the Dingle Peninsula, following many off-the-beaten-path roads to avoid the tourist traffic.

Killarney is a busy tourist center, packed with tour buses, shops, discos, and cabarets. Yet the stunning beauty of the surrounding area—a combination of heather-clad mountains, deep-blue lakes and lush vegetation—remains unspoiled. Killarney National Park, famous for its lake and mountain scenery, occupies a large part of the valley.

Light rain is typical in southwest Ireland, but it seldom lasts long. The clouds billow over the lakes or hills, showers follow, and within minutes, brilliant sunshine and rainbows emerge. During the month of April, when I biked in Ireland, there can be more rain and cooler weather than May to September. The temperature ranged from 50°-60° Fahrenheit.

In good weather, the trip to the Gap of Donloe is an idyllic bike and hike excursion from Killarney. The gap is a four-mile trail that winds along the ridge above steep gorges and five deep glacial lakes.

Leaving the Ring of Kerry, I pedaled toward the Dingle Peninsula where the movies *Ryan's Daughter* (with Sara Miles and Christopher

Jones) and *Far and Away* (with Nicole Kidman and Tom Cruise) were filmed.

The Dingle Peninsula is a meeting place of sorts, where wave-carved cliffs and rolling hills fend off a moody, restless Atlantic, and the memories of sea battles merge with the scent of wildflowers. The natural stage of the Dingle itself, often veiled in mist, enlivened by the pounding surf, is a draw for travelers in search of solitude, renewal, and natural beauty.

Many evenings, after a hard day's ride, I visited the local pub to share lively conversation and music over a pint of nut-brown Guinness. I would take a seat, call for a drink, and listen as the tune was handed on from fiddle to flute, from strings to pipe. Toe tapping began and I could feel the rhythm deepen as it went around, strengthening and gaining in confidence. I often found myself happily lost in the intricate melodies.

A green-eyed, bearded young fiddler assured me, "There isn't a corner of the country where music isn't central to the gathering. You see," he continued, "it doesn't have to be organized, and the group of musicians may change as the evening wears away." When it was late and the fingers were flying, my heart would soar.

One memorable day, after six hours of pedaling over the hills through the soft Irish mist, I heard a hiss from my front tire and knew I had a problem. It had been hours since I'd seen the sun, my leg muscles screamed, and my back end burned. My only companions, black and white cows plodding across the road, were indifferent.

Enviously, I thought about the pampered guests on the organized tours. Had I booked my trip with a bicycle company, a support vehicle and guide would have come to my rescue to repair my tire, while I joked and commiserated with my fellow cycling companions. But alone, with a leaking tire, a wet body, and a soggy spirit, I wondered if Ireland's terrain defied the laws of physics and the entire country was uphill. It was time to break for hot coffee and a warm scone–or perhaps, a reviving Guinness.

In the distance, at the crest of the next hill, I could see white cottages with gray slate roofs. Through the thin clouds one chimney rose above the others, pouring out a fragrant plume of peat smoke from a turf fire. "Ah," I thought, "that must be the village pub." After an hour of low-tire pumping, I was there.

I tramped into the pub's inviting warmth, drenched and disheveled, feeling conspicuous, but the man behind the worn wooden bar put me at ease. As he served my Guinness, he grinned and asked, "Can you sing?"

Now where else in the world would a bartender ask this question of a young lady who stood dripping water on the floor?

"Yes, I think I can sing," I answered. Lord Guinness worked his magic and loosened my tongue, and out flowed, "When Irish Eyes Are Smiling," which my half-Irish mother used to sing to me when she tucked me into bed. An elderly man in tattered tweed coat and wool cap stepped up to the bar, squared his shoulders, took a deep breath, and then belted out, "Mine eyes have seen the glory of the coming of the Lord."

Other customers left their darts and conversations to gather around us. "Sing another one, Yankee," they urged and then joined in. They knew two or three verses to each song. It's hard to stop a song session from taking shape when everyone loves to sing and it's warm inside and spitting Irish dew outside.

An hour and a dozen tunes later, when I was ready to leave, the impromptu choir members insisted on paying for my brews and then escorted me to the door. As I stepped outside—miracle of miracles—the sun was shining again.

The men stood in the door and watched me start to wrestle with my little bicycle pump, ineptly trying to fix my flat tire. With loud and teasing guffaws, they poured out of the pub and organized a work party; the baritone fetched a repair kit from his barn. As they worked, we sang another song and I passed around the last of my Cadbury chocolate bars. It didn't take them long to patch the leak, and as I pedaled off, I turned and waved. They waved back, smiles a mile wide.

Biking through a land of more rainbows than I'd ever seen in my life, over hills and through mist, pushed me physically, but my real discovery was the people. I learned that the sun in the Irish soul is expressed through song, and the smile in Irish eyes is contagious.

THE END OF THE ROAD

Alone on a camel, Marybeth travels through
the remote Indian Thar desert.

———

I always wanted to go to the end of the road. I had given up my job, and with it the career I had worked so hard to build. I had packed up my house, put all my belonging, including my car, in storage and I took off for a year-long sojourn through Asia. Now, perhaps, I could follow a road to its end.

After three painfully hot days on the train from Delhi, I saw Jaisalmer rise out of the flat, yellow Rajasthani desert like a honeycomb. From the humblest shop to the Maharaja's palace, the entire town glowed with the golden color of sandstone from which it is built. Three centuries ago Jaisalmer's location on the old camel rout between India and Central Asia had brought it great wealth. Today it is the end of the line. The air is heavy with the fragrances of jasmine, cinnamon, and sweet curries. Women in flowing scarves and saris of saffron, turquoise, and vermillion glide among the camels, sacred cows, and rickshaws in the narrow unpaved streets.

Sipping tea in an outdoor café, I was enjoying the sight of three regal Rajasthani men in white tunics and pink and orange turbans when I noticed in the square were focused on me. Feeling uncomfortable, I gulped my steaming tea and slipped into the tangled maze within the old city walls.

Traveling in the summer, in the Indian desert, I thought I had left all Americans or Europeans behind, but at dinner my second evening, I met a French couple from Paris.

Gerard was a professional photographer on his second trip to Jaisalmer. A year before, he had spend a month photographing the desert people. Now he had returned with his fiancée, Nicole, to show her his beloved landscape. Although he was very excited by the idea of returning to visit a friend, Farid, in his remote village in the Thar desert, Nicole didn't seem at all enthusiastic. She had very little to say in either French or Englis; her bewitching green eyes, framed by long black eyelashes, never stopped scrutinizing me. Gerard, on the other hand, was elated to find an enthusiastic audience for his stories. What excited him about the Thar, he said, was that people still lived exactly as they had for centuries.

Suddenly, without consulting Nicole, he asked me if I would like to accompany them on their visit to his friend's village. He added, probably without knowing, that the words themselves would tempt me, that it was at "the end of the road."

The next morning at the intersection that served as the bus stop, Gerard introduced me to Farid, then squeezed through the bus's doorway to join Nicole in a seat. The vehicle was so crammed with passengers, pigs, chickens, baskets, and oats that Farid looked at me and pointed to the roof. He formed a foothold with his hands. I caught at an open window and climbed atop the bus which was piled high with trunks, baggage, livestock, and humans. The only unoccupied space on the whole roof was on top of two filthy, spare tires. Farid smiled and shrugged as we plopped down on the hot rubber.

The bus roared out of town. The blowing sand and grit stung my face and eyes. I put on my sunglasses, and, following the example of the men around me, who used part of their red turbans to cover their mouths and noses, I wrapped my head and mouth with a scarf. The men's dark penetrating eyes were left exposed.

Clouds of dust unfurled behind us as we drove west into the desert and back into time. Sheep and goats scurried from the road. A baby camel, unsure on skinny legs, looked up from where its mother was guarding it as it ate from a single shrub that clung to a sand dune.

As we traveled deeper into the desert, I noticed that the village men were dressed more and more elegantly. They strutted about with their heads swathed in turbans. Thick black mustaches coiled on their weather-beaten cheeks. The women were no less flamboyant in brilliant, ankle-length skirts embroidered with sequins and minute mirrors that glittered as they moved. They wore tight-fitting bodices and on their foreheads, ears, noses, necks, and arms they wore silver jewelry. Women and children running out to meet their returning men were like joyous visions stepping from Moghul miniature paintings. They came to life with grace and beauty against the parched land and the mud huts. I tried to imagine what their lives were like.

As we proceeded farther and farther into the heat and vastness of the desert, the bus slowly emptied; the road became less and less defined. Upon depositing several men at a cluster of mud huts, where no women came out to greet them, Farid leaned over to tell me: "No marriages have taken place in this village for over five hundred years."

I was startled. Then, not sure I believed him, and not knowing what to say, I stared off into the desert.

"The men in this hamlet never marry. Women who have no dowry end up here to be kept as community property."

I glanced at the hamlet, then at him.

He whispered, "Like brood mares." Then he too looked off into the desert as he added matter of factly, "Female babies are suffocated at birth with a bag of salt."

I shook my head at his gruesome tale. I wanted to put my hands over my ears.

"Women who give birth to girl babies too often are also killed."

The bus started up with a lurch. I didn't want to believe Farid, but I had recently seen the tiny handprints young widows had pressed into the mud walls of the Jodhpur Fort before they burned themselves on the funeral pyres in the nineteenth century. Just a few days ago I had read in the Delhi newspaper about the many "dowry deaths" of youn girls. Wives often caught fire "accidentally" while cooking, thus freeing the husband to remarry, giving him a chance to secure a larger dowry.

We came to the end of the dirt road, not far from the Pakistani border. Ten round earth-colored huts with straw roofs clustered together against the immensity of the desert. Women, children, and barking dogs ran out to meet us. The bus soon turn around, leaving us in the dust. It sped back toward Jaisalmer.

Farid's younger brother, Abdul, greeted him with the hugs and kisses traditional among desert men, and proudly escorted us through the huts to their home. It contained a large room with open windows, several wooden cots, and a table. The jingling of tiny bells from the rings on her toes announced their mother's arrival. Her bearing was regal, and her face was uncovered. She welcomed us warmly with nods and smiles.

Exhausted from our journey, we accepted an offer to stretch out on the cots. During our rest, curious children poked their heads in at the open doors and windows, sometimes giggling, but often just staring in silence. We were more strange to them than they to us. One tiny girl peered timidly from behind the legs of an older boy to assess the strangers. When she stepped into the light I saw a long red scar that ran from the corner of her right eye to her mouth. I gasped. The older boy, who said he was her brother, told Farid that a rat had bitten her.

After a short rest, we were invited across the courtyard to a tiny, unfurnished dining room, where we sat on the floor to eat a hearty lunch of rice, lentils, and curried potatoes. There were no eating utensils so we, as the Indians did, used our right hands. After lunch Farid showed us into the family salon for tea. Shelves on the walls held flashlight batteries and empty pop bottles—rare items in the desert.

As Farid's mother served us tea, I noticed that Farid and Abdul treated her with great respect. She did not fit the stereotype I had of an exploited Muslim woman. Farid told me his father had been killed in a border skirmish years ago and his mother alone raised him and his brother. I wished I could talk to her in her own language.

When the heat abated late in the afternoon, we went out to have a look around. Cows with ribs protruding from their dried-to-leather hides roamed the dirt paths. Through half-closed doorways I could see women, children, and old men sitting in walled courtyards. Their dark eyes followed our every move.

At dusk, Gerard suggested that we walk to a small hill overlooking the water pond to photograph the village women. Nicole, saying she felt ill, declined to join us.

We heard giggles and laughter before we reached the summit of the hill from which we could see the shiny copper vessels balanced on women's heads. When they saw us they became quiet and covered their faces with their veils. They filled their vessels with the muddy water and balancing them on their heads, glided back into the desert.

After a dinner in semi-darkness (there were no candles to spare), Farid and Abdul joined us. He told us that, although the Indian-Pakistan border is officially closed, the desert people do a brisk trade in camels, cattle, goats, and food supplies as well as radios, electronic goods, arms, and drugs.

"Gerard," he continued, "was the first foreigner to come here before you. I doubt any foreigner," he was watching me closely "as ever visited the surrounding villages. Would you," he flashed me a big smile, "like to see them?"

"But how?" My voice was more eager than I expected it to be.

"By camel. There are no vehicles," Farid explained, "wheels—wagon, bicycle, or car wheels get stuck in the sand. There are no roads beyond my village."

I turned to the others, sure they, too, would want to go. Gerard was intrigued, but Nicole greeted the idea with scorn. She reminded us how uncomfortable it was even here, and how much more unpleasant it would be riding on a camel and staying in far more primitive villages. Farid said he could arrange for the camels and would ask Abdul to accompany me as guide and translator. That night the thought of a camel trip into the desert wouldn't leave my mind. After hours of pondering the possibilities, I fell into a deep sleep.

Farid woke me with the first morning light, eager to tell me his mother had sent to ask a neighbor if he would be willing to interrupt his plowing and rent his two camels to us. And Abdul, he said, had agreed to come.

The bus, I knew, would not return to this village for five days. Five days would be time enough for at least a short safari. Or would I rather stay here and listen to Nicloe complain? Five days! The idea of a solo adventure tempted me.

I was eager to move on, and yet, anxiously, I kept asking myself: Why am I doing this? If anything went wrong, there would be no one to help me. But the more difficult and frightening the journey seemed, the more alluring it became. Though I tried to be rational, I was already caught up in the romance of traveling the ancient trading route that had once been part of the Silk Road.

After dinner, while Gerard, Nicole, and I were playing cards, Farid came in to announce proudly that the neighbor had arrived with his two camels. "And the camel owner," he said, "will accompany us so he can care for his animals."

I laid down my cards. "We've planned out a circular route," Farid continued, "which will take you into some Indian villages as well as others across the border, in Pakistan."

The sun had risen just enough to cast oblique shadows across the morning haze of the desert. I clambered onto the bony back of the camel to settle on a saddle composed of padded cotton quilts and wool blankets. My limited equestrian experiences had not prepared me for riding a camel. As the beast rose, first on his back legs, I was thrown forward onto his neck.

Then as he lurched up onto all fours, the ground suddenly seemed remarkably far away. Abdul, along with the camel owner, climbed onto the other animal. They led my camel with a rope attached to a wooden peg, that pierced his nose. Our little caravan headed off into the desert. Gerard and Nicole waved. "Au Revoir! Bonne chance!"

Perspiration immediately began to collect under my sunglasses and streak down my cheeks. With every drop of moisture that ran down my neck and checks, a portion of my energy evaporated. Within an hour I was drained and numb. Scant vegetation dotted the barren hills. Each tree or bush or clump of grass, no matter how small, became a focal point for my attention. Abdul and the camelman rode in silence. From time to time we passed a turbaned farmer shuffling behind a camel and guiding a wooden plow. The desert people grow millet, Farid told me, which is ground into flour to make the flat chapitis that form the staple of the Rajasthani diet. We passed one shepherd tending a scrawny herd of sheep, a few skeletal cows, and three goats.

As we plodded the endless waves of sand, the landscape became more and more barren. My enthusiasm evaporated in the excruciating heat, in the unending wind that lashed my face with burning sand. My thoughts turned inward. Over and over again I imagined cool splashing waves rushing over my body. In reality, on camelback in the Thar desert, I remained an immobile, rocking captive. Minutes seemed like hours. I hadn't worn my watch, nor missed it, since I left San Francisco, but now I urgently wanted to know the time.

Abdul spoke little English, the camelman none. My situation might have been comical if I had not been so miserable. The sun was directly overhead when we spotted the grass roofs on the horizon. Covered from head to toe in dirt, cranky from the heat, weak from dehydration, I was angry with myself for romanticizing the awful reality of a desert camel trip. This is no fun, I finally admitted to myself as tears filled my eyes and a lump grew in my throat. I was so drained of motivation, and so uncomfortable, I couldn't imagine continuing.

The village was devoid of life. My camel stopped and growled. He wasn't happy either. As I climbed down, I was so weak I collapsed right into the dirt. Abdul came running. Gently, he helped me to sit up. My legs were stiff, my whole body hurt. I desperately needed to get out of the sum and drink liquids. Abdul led me to some shade and then he went in search of a family who might take us in and provide lunch. I watched him speak to several women. Then he returned and led me to a hospitable looking hut.

Two pairs of colorful leather slippers with turned-up toes sat by the open door. I left my plastic thongs in line with the slippers and entered. Rugs were piled in one corner, and a small fire pit occupied another. Next to the hearth, clay pots three feet high and two feet in diameter stored the family's precious water. The rugs, cooking utensils, clay pots, and two copper jugs for transporting water were the only items on the tidy dirt floor. There were no cans or bottles, no radios or TVs, no pictures, photographs, or books—no printed material at all.

An attractive, perhaps thirty-year-old woman, dressed in brilliant red, green, and yellow, fanned the fire in the semi-dark hut. Her head was not draped with a scarf nor was her face concealed. Though her hands were wrinkled and leathery, her face was smooth. I counted eighteen ivory bracelets above one elbow, and thirteen on her forearm. Heavy bone bangles adorned her ankles; her toes were decorated with two silver bells. Her nose stud identified her as a married woman; the tiers of jewelry announced her husband's wealth.

Sitting on the floor I watched her prepare the tea. She avoided looking at me. Neither of us uttered a sound. Across the cultural gap that separated us, however, I felt a kind of acceptance: I was alien but unthreatening. I would provide the family with a little extra income and I would become one of the stories she told to her friends at the well.

Fatigue overcame me, so I curled up on the floor with my pack under my head and closed my eyes. Within seconds I was dreaming of swimming deep under water. When I woke, lunch was prepared and Abdul joined us. We ate rice, curried potatoes, and hot chapattis. We ate in silence. I drank cup after cup of hot, spicy tea to replenish my liquid-starved body.

After lunch I begged Abdul to call it a day, and he, always gentle and kind, agreed. The woman cleaned up from lunch and left. I spent a quiet afternoon alone in her home reading, writing in my journal, and napping. Late in the afternoon I explored the village. As I walked among the mud huts, dogs barked and children hid. The men, I learned, were in the field plowing, and the women had to walk more than an hour each way to fill their water jubs.

At sunset when the woman of the house returned with water, she immediately began to prepare dinner. Her husband, Abdul, and the camelman joined us soon after dusk, but her four young sons remained outside. The men talked until dinner was served. The woman did not speak. Again we ate rice, chaptais, and potatoes in silence. I was being treated as a male guest, for the woman ate her meal with her children when we had finished.

Later with Abdul's help as interpreter, I complimented the woman on her exquisite jewelry. She was pleased by my attention. She joked with her husband and the men. I didn't understand her words but her humor was evident. She pointed at me and giggled. Abdul said she was teasing me because I wore no jewelry to proclaim my husband's wealth. When I said I had no husband, she indicated that she felt sorry for me. What would I do, she wanted to know, if I had no husband to give me jewelry and no dowry jewels to attract one? With a man for an interpreter, I didn't feel up to embarking on an explanation of American feminism.

What had been my saddle all day became my bed for the night. Abdul helped me spread the cotton quilts on the floor of the hut, and my pack continued to serve as my pillow. Having slept in close quarters with the local people while trekking in Nepal, I did not mind the lack of privacy. However, the lack of washing water bothered me. But knowing that the woman had already walked hours to collect water for a family of six and three guests, I was unwilling to ask for more than the small bowl allotted to me. I stared into the shallow container. Should I brush my teeth? wash my face? my pits? or quench my thirst? I dipped my toothbrush in the water, then drank the remainder.

In the morning, I was honored by the woman of the house with an invitation to help cook the chapitis over the open fire in her tiny kitchen area. I was amused to think she was probably trying to show me some useful skills which would aid in catching a husband. We left when the sun was just beginning to rise.

The nasty discomfort of the first day repeated itself, and my fascination with the small mud villages vanished. They all seemed the same. The barren dunes stretched for miles and we criss-crossed the unguarded border between Pakistan and India. I could distinguish the Moslem women from the Hindu because the Moslem women kept purdah—clothed from head to toe in black, hiding from the eyes of all men save for their families. The Rajput Hindu women, like the hostess in my first village, dressed in brilliant colors.

I thought of the lives of the Thar desert women, the status that jewelry and marriage gave them, and compared it to my determination to live my life on my own.

But alone in the Thar desert with only blue sky, and sand, and two men more silent than I, I could find no escape from the tormenting truth. As I shifted my aching bones in the saddle, I knew I alone was the one who was responsible for my maddening discomfort. It became clear to me that accepting responsibility for her acts is a rite of passage for a women. Suddenly, I realized the trip across the desert had become my rite of passage. How much could I endure?

When our camels stopped in the village where we could rest for the second night, it was already after sundown. With the last bit of my strength, I slid off the camel and stood by myself in the shadows.

Adbul and the camelman went off to arrange for fodder for the animals and dinner and lodging for us. I sat in the dirt and stared into space. It seemed like hours before Abdul returned. He apologized and said that no one was willing to allow me to sleep in their home. "A single woman," he said, "is suspect." I reminded him that I would pay well for the honor of sleeping on someone's floor, but he told me money was not the object, a family's reputation mattered more.

I settled for the flat roof of the village schoolhouse. Having climbed the primitive wooden ladder, I made my bed for the night by spreading out quilts in the corner. Abdul gave me some cold chapattis he had been carrying with him in the event of not finding food. I ate them quickly to keep the howling wind from blowing sand into my meager dinner.

A tall, powerful-looking man climbed the ladder to our rooftop and spoke to Abdul. They looked at me shaking their heads and discussing some issue of importance—perhaps Abdul had found a husband for me. But when Abdul turned to me he asked if I would like to hear some Rajasthani folk music. And would I care to taste the local "home brew?" If so, he could arrange it through this man, the village elder.

No food in the village, no place to stay, but they could play their music for me. I felt put upon, but I agreed. Eleven men wearing orange-and-red turbans came to sit in the school courtyard below my perch. One man played a hand accordion, another the *sarangi*, a violin-like instrument. I learned from Abdul's translation that the melancholy songs were about love and battles. The charm of the repetitious rhythm soon wore off, and the white lightening of the desert, called *asha*, was too strong for my taste. I crawled off to my corner of the roof to be alone.

The wind began to blow ferociously. A crescent moon stood out in the pitch black sky. The stars seemed to compete with each other for space in the heavens. I was awed by the beauty of the desert night, but pleasure lay shrouded beneath fatigue and loneliness. Despite the suffocating heat, I huddled under my quilt to protect myself from the blowing sand, and dust, and tried to sleep. The entire sand floor of the desert seemed to be shifting across my bed. I could still hear the village men singing and enjoying themselves as I finally slipped off to sleep.

Danger! I struggled out of sleep. The crescent moon had set, the wind had stopped blowing, the night was dark and silent. I lay dead still, my heart pumping in my chest and a lump of fear rising in my throat. Someone was pulling on my cotton quilt. I smelled alcohol. A big cold hand touched my bottom. Terrified, then infuriated, I kicked backward, hitting the soft part of a body with my heel. At the same time I slapped over my head with one arm and screamed at the top of my voice, "Leave me alone!"

I flipped over to face my assailant. I could make out the shadow of the camelman as he crept across the roof and descended the wooden ladder. Where was Abdul? Despote the hear and the weight of my quilts, I began to shiver. Don't be hysterical, I reprimanded myself. Forget it. Go back to sleep. I was lucky, after all, that the camelman was a timid soul, for I was in no shape to fight off a determined attacker. As I kept shaking, I began to pray: "Our father, Who art in heaven . . ."

The camelman understood my cold glare and cool attitude for the remained of the trip. Abdul realized something had happened, became more conscientious as my bodyguard. No further incidents occurred.

The third day as we entered one more village, where I was looking forward to a little exercise to work out the pain in my legs, only dogs came out to bark. But I could partly see and partly intuit that, as in other villages, eyes were scrutinizing us from behind the almost-closed shutters and doors.

As Abdul descended from his camel, a group of men converged on us. shouting "Pagal, Pagal." One old man with a rifle threatened to shoot. Abdul did not utter a word, but, rapidly remounting, he prodded our animals to move quickly out of town. The men followed, screaming insults until we were far beyond their boundaries. The villagers felt, Abdul spoke softly, that a woman traveling alone could only mean trouble. Such a woman must be either a lunatic or a witch. They wanted no part of me and my bad luck. My mood was such that, I felt it almost an honor, a compliment, to be labeled mad and banished as a witch. I had had just about enough of questioning my own value.

Since Abdul wanted to avoid villages where he didn't personally know a family, we were forced to camp on the sand dunes the last two nights. Before retiring, Abdul scattered raw onion around. "It'll keep the pena at bay," he said.

"What's pena?" I asked.

"It's a snake that comes at night and crawls onto your warm chest. It spits venom into your nostrils and lashes its tail across your face." Fear of the pena didn't keep me awake. I was too tired to care.

On our last day, I caught a glimpse of two wild gazelle with twisted horns playing spiritedly in the distance, and I saw a single man in an orange turban, his back straight and his head held high, walking behind a camel. Arriving back in Abdul's village, we stopped at the water hole to give the camels a drink. The women, hearing us approach, ran to the opposite side of the pond. They giggled and pointed at me.

Abdul's mother welcomed us with genuine warmth and visible relief. I was happy to be back in the village at the end of the road connected to civilization by motorized transportation.

Beyond the end of the road, despite the swirling sand, howling wind, and overpowering heat, I had come to appreciate the austere beauty of the desert. I was filled with wonder, that, out there, I had discovered serenity in solitude and spiritual peace.

MARRAKECH MAMA

Learning to shed extra baggage is a mother's dilemma.

———

My career involves frequent travel and often for extended periods, making me vulnerable to self-doubt and guilt. I often question my role as a parent. Was I a good mother? A good enough mother? Was my babysitter the best available? Did my husband resent the extra work at home while I was away? With every trip, I packed and hauled along extra baggage. Shouldered every mile, along with my duffels, totes, and briefcase, I dragged this heavy load of doubt and reproach. The quiet claws of uncertainty became a constant part of my planning, packing, and leave-taking for years. The pain of separation and concern about my family's well-being clouded the joy of taking off for those new worlds I was supposed to be exploring.

When my flights left early in the morning. I would tiptoe into my children's bedroom to say my silent goodbyes while they were still fast asleep, inhaling the familiar fragrance of shampoo in their silken hair, nuzzling my nose into their soft, warm necks, and running my fingers over their downy cheeks. Then I would burst into tears on the way to the airport.

The intensity of my goodbyes varied with every trip. I learned that leaving a sick child or being absent for more than one weekend took the heaviest emotional toll. I suffered one of my worst bouts of guilt when my daughters were three and six years old and I went to Morocco for seventeen days on business—the longest I had ever been away from home. But, it was that very trip that ultimately freed me and put my life back into perspective.

For weeks before my departure for North Africa I took extra precautions to keep every microbe away from my children. Compulsively I spent every free moment playing with them. I made endless lists and schedules for my husband and the babysitter, stocked the cupboards and refrigerator to overflowing, and filled "goodie bags" with simple, gift-wrapped treats to be opened each day I was away. But even my best efforts didn't alleviate my guilt.

Although the pain of separation faded slowly with the excitement of experiencing Africa, I still felt stabs of guilt each day. To comfort myself and stay emotionally connected to home I carried pictures of my family with me everywhere and enthusiastically shared them with waitresses, guides, and travel companions. I safety-pinned my favorite snapshots to the canvas walls of my tent when camping in the Sahara Desert. One day I pulled them out of my backpack to share with a nomadic Bedouin woman and her newborn baby as she boiled water for tea over a wood fire. Together we smiled and cooed over her child and my pictures.

In Marrakech, I placed a framed picture of my daughters on the bedside table in my hotel room, as had become my custom. For years I had performed the same nesting ritual in every hotel, in every city: I would throw open the curtains for light, mess up the covers on the bed, and ceremoniously place framed snapshots of my children and husband all over the room. Perched on the night-stand, inches from my head, the smiles of my daughters would soothe me as I fell asleep.

I thought of them constantly, and shopping for treasures to take home filled the small amount of free time I had on my first day in the city. In the bustling, colorful alleys of the medina I bargained for tiny embroidered slippers with turned-up toes, leather camels, and exotic dolls. Finally, exhausted from the noonday heat, I returned to the oasis of my hotel room, eager for a few minutes of silence and a cool shower. But, when I unlocked the door I immediately smelled flowers. In a moment I saw them. There, around the picture of my children, fragrant roses had been arranged, transforming the bedside table into a beautiful altar with offerings. But from whom? This touching but mysterious ritual continued for two days. Magically, fresh flowers kept appearing to adorn my children's smiles.

On my last day in Morocco I returned to the hotel late in the afternoon. As I stepped out of the elevator, I heard a rustling in the hall. A short woman with flashing brown eyes and a charcoal-colored bun quickly pushed aside her maid's cart and hurried to greet me. She had obviously been waiting for this moment. Motioning me closer with her keys, she unlocked my door. As I followed her into the room I was once again struck by the sweet smell of flowers. The new offerings were red, white, and pink carnations.

The woman led me to the bedside table where she lovingly lifted the picture of my daughters to her chest and held it tightly. Then she raised the frame to her lips and kissed each girl's photo. I pointed to the flowers, bowed my head, and tried to express my thanks with my hands pressed together in the universal gesture of prayer. Smiling, the woman then pulled a crumpled photograph of her own family from her apron pocket. I took it, admired her four children, then held the picture to my chest and embraced it as she had, gently kissing each child. I reached out to touch her arm in appreciation, and she hugged me closely. As we stood embracing in silent female communion, tears filled my eyes and my throat choked closed with emotion.

Using only gestures and our eyes and smiles, we told each other about our children, and I felt blessed and quietly at peace. This was the true reward of travel: not the places visited but the people who have touched my life. This compassionate Muslim woman reminded me once again that mothers all over the world work, out-side the home, and are thus separated from their children by that work. It is not a choice for most of them, or for most of us. And we are not bad mothers because of it.

In that brief moment of sharing family pictures in a strange city so far from home, I realized that nothing has ever made me as happy or as sad as Motherhood. And that nothing has ever been quite as hard, as intense, or as satisfying.

Occasionally in my travels I experience something that forever alters my life, that brings me back a changed person. So it was in a quiet room in Marrakech. Despite my homesickness, a generous Moroccan mother helped me replace guilt with gratitude forever.

GUARDIANS OF THE NIGHT

*A mother worries about safety living in Mexico
with her young daughters.*

———

"Are you scared, Mommy?" whispered my seven-year-old daughter in the back seat of the battered Mexican taxi.

The driver accelerated, swerving into the left lane to pass a farm truck full of cows. The pale hazy sun slipped behind the mountains. Night was descending quickly as we roared through the desert toward San Miguel de Allende; it would be dark before we arrived.

More than the forced smile on my face, my queasy stomach spoke the truth. I was very nervous about our maniac driver, the lack of seatbelts, and how long it was taking us to get to San Miguel.

Annalyse, the seven-year-old, squeezed my hand, snuggling her head into my shoulder. She thinks I am invincible, I thought with a sense of irony. Her mom, the author of "Gutsy Women," felt like an un-gutsy wimp. I could be so brave when I was alone, but add the responsibility of traveling with my daughters and I was having an attack of insecurity.

I avoided an honest answer and rationally, if not confidently, responded, "Sweetie, whenever I travel somewhere I've never been before, I'm both excited and uncomfortable."

I explained, "I am just wondering what our host family will be like. During meals together will we be able to communicate? We don't know very much Spanish do we? I bet they don't know much English either. I hope our teachers at the Language Institute will be as nice as your first-grade teacher this past year."

In the silence that filled the dark cab, I realized for the first time this trip wouldn't be easy. I wished there was another grown-up along to help me keep an eye on my exuberant, wandering blond daughters.

Why was I so insecure about going to Mexico alone with my kids? Before marriage and motherhood I had traveled alone around the world for two years. I used to be a confident traveler. Motherhood seemed to have made me wary and cautious.

I could blame it on traveler's fatigue. We were exhausted, having survived three flights to get to Mexico City. The flight was "direct," but of course the airline never mentioned the two stopovers along the way!

News programs in the United States had warned us about the violent crime in and outside the Mexico City Airport. We held hands to stay together in the crowded terminals. Julieclaire and I wore our backpacks over our chests, instead of on our backs, to thwart pickpockets and thieves.

Outside the terminal there were no benches for weary travelers at the curbside bus stop, so we stood waiting for over an hour for the bus to Quaretaro. I was exhausted from watching our luggage, protecting my children and keeping them entertained.

Aboard the Primera Plus deluxe bus, Julieclaire and Annalyse napped. I nervously thumbed guidebooks during the four-hour trip. At the bus stop, we hailed a cab for the one-hour journey to our final destination, a Mexican home in San Miguel de Allende.

The scrubby countryside of the highlands of central Mexico ended abruptly as we drove into town. We passed tacky-looking shops and bars with men spilling onto the unpaved streets. Where were the traffic lights, the neon signs and fast food establishments I saw in other Mexican towns?

Our cabbie stopped twice to ask for directions. Where were the narrow cobbled-stone streets and the charming colonial villas described in the guidebooks? When we careened around a corner into a dirt alley I was sure we were lost or being taken for a ride.

Our decrepit cab lurched to a stop as the grizzled driver pointed with pleasure at a messy hand-written sign on a white washed wall. It was the street address I had given him. I slumped back in stunned silence.

This neighborhood had no reassuring streetlights, no pedestrians, trees or even a stray barking dog. It was deserted and dirty. When he found the house address, my stomach churned. I didn't want to get out of the taxi. The darkness, silence and poverty of the scene were intimidating.

The cabbie wanted no part of my hesitation or insecurities. He dumped our luggage on the street, grabbed his pesos and sped off.

We pounded on the wooden door and hoped for the best. Annalyse's tiny warm hand found its way into my clammy cold fist. Julieclaire impatiently scuffed her foot in the dirt.

A short woman with charcoal-colored hair threw open the door, grabbed my free hand and pumped it in an energetic greeting. She was wearing a starched white apron over a somber black dress. Her unlined face made me guess she was in her thirties.

She introduced herself as Lourdes, and wasted no time welcoming Annalyse and Julieclaire with hugs. Julieclaire, at ten-years-old, was almost as tall as Lourdes. She took charge, leading us through an empty garage and into the main house, chattering non-stop in staccato Spanish. Her monologue, none of which we understood, cheered us up as we stacked our heavy luggage in a corner of our new home for the next fifteen days.

Lourdes knew intuitively what we needed. My children were hungry and I wanted to be taken care of. She led us into a large, empty dining room and seated us at the only piece of furniture, a lace-covered table.

She brought in bowls of corn flakes and cold milk. Ah, reassuring corn flakes! I remembered another time, when I had been on the road for over nine months, alone. I discovered corn flakes on a restaurant menu in Southern India. I relished every bite, transported back to Ohio and childhood breakfast before school.

Corn flakes had been my emotional link with home. And now, lifetimes later, my daughters also found a bowl of familiar cereal reassuring.

Removing her apron, Lourdes smoothed down her glossy hair, smiled and sat down at the table with us. Little Patrick, her cheerful five-year-old son, climbed onto her lap and furtively glanced at the girls. He made funny faces to get their attention. Julieclaire made goofy faces in return and our laughter echoed through the bare rooms.

After our snack, Annalyse and Julieclaire argued over who would get the bigger drawer in the dresser for their clothes; and over who had to sleep with mom on which bed in our tiny dark bedroom. Patrick peeked through the half-open door. He was fascinated by these two foreign girls who were squabbling as they pulled hair bows and games out of their bags.

Meanwhile, Lourdes gave me a tour of her three bedroom, cement block home, showing me what I would need to know—how to use the key to lock the front door, where to find purified water to refill our water bottles for drinking and brushing teeth.

We climbed up a narrow set of chipped cement stairs to the flat roof that served as the laundry. Lourdes showed me the clotheslines where we should hang our damp towels. A big, enamel wash tub, with a wooden washboard and bars of soap stood in the corner. This is where I would hand wash our clothes and hang them up to dry.

Wooden clothespins held sheets and underwear on the clotheslines. They flapped in the balmy summer breeze. A crescent moon was pasted against the black velvet sky. A myriad of stars competed with each other for space in the heavens. I was awed by this nocturnal beauty but pleasure lay shrouded beneath fatigue and sobering maternal responsibility.

Lourdes held back the corner of a drying sheet and motioned for me to follow her through the laundry to the other side of the open roof. I was unprepared for the sight that awaited me. Dominating the city's panorama was a pink Gothic cathedral with ornate steeples aglow with tiny lights.

We could hear the children below, giggling together in the bedroom. They were playing peekaboo. I let out a sigh of relief.

Lourdes spoke to me in slow sentences. My knowledge of French helped me to piece together her Spanish words. Lourdes was divorced, living alone with her children. She supported them taking in language students as boarders.

In addition to Patrick, she had a twenty-year-old son who worked the night shift in a dry cleaning factory and an eighteen-year-old daughter who was still in school and spent most of her time with her "novia," or boyfriend. With a shrug and resigned laugh, she explained that her older children were rarely at home.

Lourdes attended elementary school for four years and could read and write "a little." She considered herself fortunate, because after her divorce, she kept the house but little else. Now I understood why the rooms were sparsely furnished. Julieclaire noticed there were no pictures on the walls and not a book to be seen in the home.

When Lourdes finished speaking I wanted to tell her about my family, my life. Many times in my travels I have confided in other women, often relative strangers. I have told them secrets about my loves, my losses, my insecurities. Under the regal moon, Lourdes and I stood in silent female communion and I tried to explain my fear.

I pointed to the dark, empty streets below and asked her in my schoolbook Spanish: "I am with my daughters. My husband, their Papa, is not with us. No other adult is with us. Is it possible to walk in the streets at night? We want to go after dinner to the main square, to sit on the wrought-iron park benches near the bandstand to watch people or hear the mariachis play, to see the peddlers offering candy and the old men get their shoes shinned. But there are no lights here."

I motioned to the dark and deserted street below and continued, "No one is in the streets. I am afraid. Is it a problem? Is my purse safe? Are my girls safe?"

Lourdes reached out and looped her arm through mine. She was small but solid and smelled as fresh as her hand-scrubbed clothing that hung around us. As we stood arm in arm, amid the fluttering laundry, I knew she understood my distress.

She pointed to a nearby rooftop. I saw two women rocking in chairs quietly conversing as they watched the streets below. They were partially hidden by their own drying laundry. I was surprised, for I hadn't noticed any other life in the neighborhood.

She motioned to other roofs and open windows where women were together, witnesses to the dark and silent night. "No problem, Senora. Many women watch out for you. No problem to walk in the streets at night with no man," she assured me.

I had traveled to San Miguel to experience the customs and the language, but the lasting legacy of our journey was this female kinship, this reaffirmation of the bond our gender feels, worldwide, as we confide in and support each other.

My daughters and I learned some Spanish, shared in another family's life, walked confidently in the dark, laughed at ourselves, and ate too much ice cream.

Most importantly, we returned home, forever changed, surer of ourselves, strengthened, stretched, and having touched other women with our spirits.

GIRLS ADVENTURING IN
NAVAJO COUNTRY

Go at your own pace, find activities to interest everyone.

———

"Campfire smoke rising up the canyon walls, stars overhead, and a full belly—what more could you want?" our Navajo guide asked us. I glanced at my two daughters, huddled close to the blazing fire, and nodded. Maybe it was the aspirin I had taken to soothe my screaming muscles, or the endorphins surging through my veins from hours of bumping and lurching in the saddle, or perhaps I was completely content to be with my daughters in the Arizona wilderness. There were no phones, no electricity, and no paved roads where we were camped deep in Mystery Canyon on the Navajo Tribal Lands.

Nearby, the horses shuffled and munched their oats under a juniper tree. Silent and mysterious Anasazi ruins loomed on the high ledges above and the fire cast eerie shadows on the red rock canyon walls.

While we sat around the glowing campfire, sated from a traditional trail feast of streaks, salad and baked potatoes, Gunnar, Evelyn's son, and our guide, created a drum from a plastic bucket and wrapped tissue paper around the end of a stick. He drummed and sang traditional Navajo songs about honor, eagles, war, and romance. My nine and twelve-year-old daughters were mesmerized by his melodious, haunting voice. I watched their glowing faces in the dancing firelight as the music seeped into my soul. The spontaneous concert and awesome grandeur of the ancient canyon enveloped us under a black velvet sky laden with brilliant stars.

Evelyn, a former bank manager, now runs a Navajo Trading Post outside Monument Valley and has the only female-owned trail riding company in the area. She's an organized, competent and big-hearted businesswoman and a forty-six-year old grandma. "Mom's one of those people who is happiest in the saddle," her son Gunner told us.

I discovered Evelyn's tour company online and signed us up for two days of horseback riding and camping in Mystery Valley, adjacent to Monument Valley.

Each day during a four-hour trail ride, Evelyn told us about growing up in a traditional Navajo Hogan; a circular domed structure made of mud and logs. On her second birthday her mother balanced her in the saddle, told her to hold on while they herded sheep from the high mesa to the lowland pastures.

Annalyse trotted on a magnificent quarter horse, Hoskinini, named after the last prominent Navajo chief, who defied the troops of Kit Carson. JC galloped full speed across the dusty meadows, then turned around and galloped back to us. I sauntered along the trail, taking time to breathe in the sagebrush-scented air. Puffy white clouds were streaked with pink; the reflected color from the crimson rocks.

Our leisurely pace gave us time to absorb the spectacular landscapes and to imagine what it was like to be an Indian on horseback tracking antelope through these canyons.

We stopped often to examine elaborate geometric petroglyphs juxtaposed with detailed hunting scenes near the ruins of the prehistoric Anasazi Indians who lived in this area for 1,000 years until they mysteriously disappeared about 1300 A.D. Our favorite pueblo ruin was "House of Many Hands"—so named because the cliff walls were covered with tiny hand prints.

Although I enjoy adventure travel, I worried about the rigors of horseback riding all day with nine and twelve-old-year old girls and camping every night. My concerns were unfounded. They loved the riding and exploring and we slept well thanks to thick double sleeping bags and cots.

Family vacations don't get much better than this. Everyone got something they wanted. JC, "the teen" had adrenaline rushes and earned "bragging rights" for galloping full speed across the plains. Annalyse was thrilled to discover fossilized dinosaur tracks and prong-horned antelope petroglyphs etched into the canyon walls by the Anasazi. And I was thrilled to spend quality time with my girls to ride horses, explore the great outdoors and learn about the Navajo.

The lasting legacy of the journey was our personal relationship with Evelyn and her son. Now the Navajo people, history and stories are real to us. And we experienced the West the way it has been explored for centuries: on horseback and sleeping under the stars.

FAMILY SAFARI

There's more to an African safari than observing wildlife.

———

The noise was wild and untamed—the primeval voice of Africa herself. The full-chested roars of two male lions echoed across the plain, striking terror into their prey and pumping adrenaline into our veins. Nine-year old Annalyse slipped her tiny hand into mine and squeezed it. I squeezed back with a sweaty palm. Naturally our first reaction was fear. After all, my husband, two daughters and I were in a Land Rover with our torsos emerging from the open roof, nothing more than fifty yards and a jeep door between us and these fierce predators. We were close enough to see their individual whiskers and piercing amber eyes. The two males continued to greet each other with verbal ferocity as the morning air vibrated with their deep vocalizations. "I guess we're not in Kansas anymore," whispered our sarcastic twelve-year-old J.C. "Keep quiet and don't make any quick movements. They haven't had breakfast yet," Tanzanian guide Leonard said with the hint of a smile. Instructions understood; we remained still and silent, in heart-pounding proximity to the lions that strutted and stretched in the orange luminescence of the rising sun.

Soon our bellies growled and we headed back to camp for our own meals. Every day we kept a tally of the animals we saw; in addition to the lions, we watched twenty-one elephants ambling to the watering hole from all directions, leaping impala (we clapped for their high jumps), two loping hyenas, four comical wart hogs zigzagging through the grass with their tails pointing skyward, and dozens of zebra and Thomson's gazelles—all before a hearty breakfast of scrambled eggs and cinnamon buns.

In our household we read every National Geographic Magazine with awe and envy. The stories and compelling photos of African wildlife as well as the discoveries of early man at Olduvai Gorge in the Rift Valley motivated us, as a family, to put Africa at the top of our travel list. I developed a sense of urgency when I read this phrase in a travel magazine: Tanzania is to wildlife, what Florence is to western art. My husband and I believe that the nuances of European art, architecture and history cannot be appreciated by young children. However, the pre-teen years are the perfect time to take a family safari in Africa.

Each day at dawn and again late in the afternoon we joined our Tanzanian guide and driver in a safari-ready land rover, and headed into the bush. Careening around termite mounds, up steep banks and down rutted slopes, we watched wildlife from a breathtakingly close vantage point. Sometimes we stayed with them even as they closed in on prey, other times we came upon them just after a kill.

The kids adored Leonard, the Pied Piper of African guides. They listened eagerly as he shared his extensive knowledge about the local mammals, birds and history of the Great Rift Valley; from Tarangire National Park to Olduvai Gorge, and the Serengeti to the Norgorogora Crater.

Prior to our African vacation we thought observing the big animals would be the zenith of our trip, however the camaraderie with our guides, and numerous contacts with the local people were equal highlights. One day we had lunch with Gebra, our Chagga guide, and his family in their home. Another day we visited a Masaai village where the homes were made of cow dung, the women wore massive bead necklaces, flies buzzed overhead and hovered around the children's eyes. The village chief, wealthy enough to have two wives, took my husband aside for a private conversation, in which he offered him two goats for our oldest daughter.

Both girls kept safari journals. JC wrote, "Right before dinner we sneaked up to the roofless shower tent where Leonard was showering. We got a bucket of ice, filled it with cold water and I stood on a stool and dumped it over the top onto him. It was hilarious! He screeched and swore. It was awesome."

"I drove for the first time today—across the Serengeti! Leonard took me out in the land rover and when I took the wheel we jerked and bumped through the grass. Mom and Dad applauded from the porch of their tent. It was so cool!"

On another page she described our visit to a country school where they met the pen pals they corresponded with for several months.

"Children attend this school because their parents are wealthy enough to spare them from working at home. Most of them walk two miles or more each way and they consider themselves lucky. And no one complains! The small kids were scared of us. One child touched my arm, then ran and hid behind his teacher. It wasn't long before they were showing us around. Hollow cement block rooms with wood benches passed as classrooms and the wild outdoors served as a bathroom. Teachers stored the text-books in their office where they were proudly displayed. Then we all played soccer together. They played barefooted in their starched blue skirts and white blouses and barefooted. We wore our special athletic shoes and they still pummeled us."

"I was very impressed with Tanzania. The people were gracious and kind. Comparing myself to those who had so little showed me how lucky I really am."

SURVIVING THE THAILAND TSUNAMI

Anything can happen.

———

My family and I couldn't wait to vacation in Southern Thailand where the weather is almost always sunny and deliciously warm. The ocean is calm and clear. That's where my husband, two daughters and I joined many other North Americans, Europeans and Australians

We had plans to snorkel, dive, sail, kayak and relax. We had no idea we were headed towards the worst natural disaster in modern times.

In October, I crossed my fingers as I planned and booked our holiday trip to Thailand—admittedly very late for such a popular warm weather destination. I was disappointed when there was "no room at the inn" along the pristine Phuket beaches, in Krabi or on Phi Phi Island. So I booked a short stay on Samui Island, located in the protected Gulf of Thailand, where we'd spend a few days and then get back to our original itinerary on the Phuket beaches and Phi Phi Island.

We flew into Phuket as planned and stayed along the popular west coast for one night before we flew back to the protected island of Ko Samui. Three days later, the Asian tsunami struck the Phuket beach where we had stayed, beach, toppling buildings, crushing and drowning thousands of tourists.

We watched the horror unfold on BBC, the only English speaking station on our hotel TV. We were a short thirty-minute flight away from the hardest hit disaster area. Thankfully, where we were staying in Ko Samui was untouched by the tsunami.

It does not bear thinking about what would have happened to us if we'd have been in Phuket as originally planned. I believe our lives were spared because there was "no room at the inn."

It took a while before the significance of the news settled in. For instance, it was my routine that every morning before my family awoke I would take a long walk along the white-sand beaches. Before breakfast, JC, our sixteen-year-old daughter, jogged at the water's edge. "She could have gone for a run and never come back. Or you could have done your morning walk and been washed out to sea," speculated my husband.

Many things "could have happened," but they didn't. Why not? Was it chance? Luck? The will of God? Or was it as simple as being in the right place at the right time?

We met many survivors over the next week. Through their eyes we saw the nightmare, and we began to realize just how close we had come to tragedy. One hundred and fifty sea-ravaged and bloated bodies washed up on the very beach where we would have been swimming, walking and jogging. We had missed it by twenty-four hours.

Flying low, over beaches littered with debris, we returned to the Phuket airport and quickly realized we could not expose our children to an 8-hour lay-over in an area that resembled a war zone. Relief workers in military fatigues, search and rescue dogs, patched and bandaged survivors filled the halls. Tragedy hung in the air like a thick layer of fog.

There were "Missing People" signs covering every wall of the terminal, posted by loved ones and officials. We saw relief workers and army helicopters searching the nearby beaches. It was the small blond, blue-eyed Scandinavian children peering out from missing person posters that haunted me the most. Each one of them seemed to resemble my own beautiful daughters who, miraculously, were safe. We were all safe.

Filling the crowded airport there were temporary booths representing different countries offering help to locate loved ones. "Missing Persons: Germany." "Missing Persons: Australia." "Missing Persons: Sweden." It went on and on.

I asked one representative at an information desk, "What nice hotel, within a thirty-minute taxi drive is somewhat intact?" Information was key and she had numerous recommendations. We ended up at the JW Marriot, an ultra-deluxe property with "limited tsunami damage."

I spoke with a British mother who had been on the beach with her ten-year-old daughter when the tsunami hit. The young girl was so traumatized that she could do no more than stare at us with her thumb in her mouth, trembling.

Our experience and the images we saw were difficult at best. Will this experience stop us from traveling? No. We love to travel because we have curiosity as well as the desire to see and connect with other cultures. When we travel, we bring home a bit of the world. We know how important it is to care for our brothers and sisters, worldwide, regardless of religion or politics.

Today, I count my blessings as I struggle to cope with our survival and the death of so many innocent people. The earth can tremble and we can vanish in an instant. Life is fragile.

But when asked, "Would you return to Thailand?" I answer unequivocally, "Absolutely, tomorrow, given the opportunity."

RETURNING TO PARADISE

Life, liberty, and the pursuit of happiness.

———

This was all my idea. And there were many moments before we boarded the twenty-five-hour flight for Bali via Taiwan when I thought I was crazy. Like when our fourteen-year-old daughter, J.C., announced we just *had* to get a hotel with a pool and internet access so she could lounge by day and email her friends by night. Or when eleven-year-old Annalyse whined, "Why can't we just go to a beach near home?"

But I wanted to return to the island paradise I had discovered twenty years before husband and children filled my life. Yes, I had been warned: "When you get a taste of island paradise, enjoy it once, because you can't return. It will never be as good." I knew the risks of returning, yet memories of Bali, seductive as a Siren's call, were luring me back to this gracious isle beyond the South Pacific.

Traveling with backpack and on a slim budget, I visited Bali the first time when I was traveling alone around the world. On the crowded, touristy beach in Kuta, I met another woman who was traveling alone. We agreed to flee the commercial coast and whoop it up cruising by motorcycle on the roller coaster of dirt roads along the northern shore and up to the base of the volcanoes. Along the way, we kept a wary eye out for the lethargic cows and dogs reluctant to give up their comfy spots in the middle of the road.

In the hills outside Ubud, we negotiated narrow footpaths amid terraced rice fields to a remote and simple guest home. The elderly owners, Katoot and Naoman, were childless, a great tragedy for a Balinese couple. "God gave us you—our young visitors—instead," they said. "You are our children to watch over and to make happy,"

At night the croaking frogs in the irrigation ditches lulled us to sleep. For breakfast, Katoot, our host mother, brought us fresh homemade yogurt with sliced papaya and mango. We spent our days bumping along dirt paths on our motorcycle, visiting local festivals, temples, artists' workshops, and even an elaborate cremation. At night, Katoot gave us long massages while our host father,

Naoman, softly played his gamelan for our pleasure. Our guestroom had no running water or shower, so we bathed like the locals, in a steep valley under a waterfall, during the morning "ladies hour."

That was my first trip to Bali, and years later, as a wife, and mother it was to Bali that I longed to return. I wanted my family to experience it paradise too.

Bali's charm, I knew, lies not in its beaches, towering volcanic mountains, or luscious green terraced rice fields, but in its people. For me, paradise could only be captured a second time if my family and I got to know and were welcomed by the Balinese.

I didn't search for Katoot or Naoman or try to recreate the same experiences. They belong to another trip, another age, a closed photo album in my mind.

We decided to pamper ourselves and the girls and stay in a luxury hotel at Jimbaran Bay, a wonderful relief after the long trans-Pacific flights and layovers. J.C. and Annalyse gave it a "thumbs-up" after they checked out the TV, video collection, free internet access, and ocean view from their own villa. They fought over who would sleep on which Balinese bed (under mosquito nets), they raced each other to jump into the private plunge pool, and denuded the tropical garden of melon-sized, pink hibiscus flowers to wear in their hair. They quickly discovered the main pool with its infinity-edge (water cascaded over a fall to soaking pools and hot and cold whirlpools below). They soaked or swam in each pool before making their way to the beach. We found them lounging by the water's edge and bribed them with mango milk shakes into joining us for a catamaran sail around the bay. Then we switched to boogie boards to surf in the large waves.

A successful family vacation offers something for everyone every day. Dad read a novel in the shade on the beach. Mom took an Asian cooking class and learned how to cook with lemon grass and Thai basil, and prepare Hot and Sour Prawn Soup, goyza, and soba noodles. The teens alternated between watching videos on the TV, body surfing, playing in the pools, getting their hair braided in cornrows and painting their nails. One afternoon we hired a driver and car to take us to a crowded, commercial beach so the girls could go parasailing. They loved it, we tolerated it. We bought elaborate, colorful kites in the shape of majestic ships and tried to fly them along the beach.

We were enjoying a different paradise than the budget Bali I had discovered and grown to love two decades before. But then, I am a different person now. Much of my own pleasure now comes from seeing my children and husband happy.

Yet I couldn't help but wonder whether the charming old Bali of decades ago still existed. If so, I knew we had to get away from the deluxe resorts and the beach to find it.

Unlike my first trip to Bali, motorcycle travel today is considered very dangerous for tourists due to the chaotic and dense traffic on the roads. If we wanted to explore the island and stay in more modest and authentically Balinese lodging, we would need a driver. You can hire a driver and car from your hotel, the local tourist office, or simply choose one of the many drivers waiting on the side of the road.

We wanted a driver who spoke good English, so he could show us his Bali and stay with us as we traveled around the island. We chose Made (mah-day) who met us at our hotel and became a part of our family for the next week. He was personable, kind, and patient; his English was good enough to help us with any situation. We shared dinner, dominoes, jokes, and stories every night. With Made at the wheel of the minivan borrowed from his older brother, we were a multicultural family. It was easy for Made to find a hotel room near ours every night, for which we paid. Together we tromped through markets, visited temples, and ate in local thatch-roofed restaurants where Made knew the owner, the cook, and the waitress. Together we ate leisurely meals in lush gardens filled with carvings and statues of frogs, gods, and goddesses. The girls sipped fresh mango smoothies, munched on satay, fried noodles, and pizza, while we feasted on the Indonesian rice table, with duck roasted in banana leaves, prawns, and spicy curries. We ventured out to the north shore to dive and snorkel on the protected coral reefs of the West Bali National Park. Amid a dervish of rainbow-colored fish we glimpsed lion fish and shark.

Best of all, Made liked us and invited us into his life and home. Outside the bustling artists' village of Ubud, he took us to see the "real Bali" that I had so longed to visit again. With Made in the lead, we trekked along steep slopes, through a maze of frog-green rice fields, down to a muddy river where young boys were bathing and women were digging sand from the riverbed to be used in construction; shoveling it into baskets, they carried the sand on their heads up the gorge. When the young boys first saw our teenage girls, they held their hands over their private parts and stared. Soon they returned to their play and ignored us passing on the rope and bamboo suspension bridge above them.

We climbed up a steep slope, through banana groves, mango, coffee, and cocoa trees to Made's village where we were treated as honored guests. His mother wore the traditional long Balinese skirt and her best Maidenform bra. "Why doesn't she wear clothes?" asked JC. "She's wearing more than she usually does, just for us," I replied.

Our hostess brought us leaf mats to sit on while we watched Made's barefoot, bare-chested uncle shimmy up a nearby coconut tree with a machete. We watched him grapple with the branches until, half an hour later, he descended with three perfectly ripe coconuts. He lopped off the tops with his machete and offered us a refreshingly cool drink of coconut milk.

Made's aunt quietly came out of the kitchen with three delicate bamboo trays filled with rice, purple bougainvillea, and fragrant frangipani flowers. She gently laid these small offerings at the base of stone statues outside the family temple. Made explained that Balinese women make and give offerings numerous times each day. This offering was made after food was cooked but before the meal was enjoyed.

This simple gesture, I thought, embodies the spirit of Bali that pervades the island. Their culture surrounds you, in the music, dance, and religion. You see it in Balinese faces, you feel it in Balinese dances.

Later in the day we drove to see one of the most important ceremonial events in Balinese culture—the cremation of a body. Regretfully, we missed the ceremony by a day, so Made, terribly upset to see us disappointed offered to take us to the wedding of his close friend. At the Balinese wedding we were seated on chairs like royal guests. Well-dressed women and men insisted we take their seats in the front rows. An elderly woman sitting next to

Annalyse smiled, nodded, and took her hand and gently held it in her lap during the ceremony. After recovering from her initial surprise Annalyse quietly responded with nods and smiles.

We were served snacks, of peanuts and chips and soft drinks. When the religious ceremony was over, the tiny, beautiful bride and her groom came to welcome us and chat.

On the twenty-five-hour journey back to the USA, I thought about our daily lives at home. So dominated by routines, job stresses, and the different demands of each child, we can easily lose perspective on what is most important to us.

When traveling, my husband and girls and I converge back into the core of this magical relationship that is family. In Bali we depended on each other for guidance, help, and fun. We got to know each other better, as well as the gracious Balinese people. And when we returned home, all was new, and we were closer and more connected.

Now I know paradise can be revisited. I saw it through the eyes of my children. Fourteen-year-old J.C. summed it up when she said, "Everyone here takes happy pills. Let's take some home."

I guess we did.

CHALLENGE AND CHARITY

The daughter now leads the mother.

———

One small word, "yes," started an avalanche of change in my life. "Yes, JC, let's ride our bikes from California to Virginia.

It seemed an overwhelming task to get in shape but one hour and one day at a time, I trained and grew more confident. One morning as I brushed my teeth, I gazed up at the mirror. What gazed back at me was a surprise; I no longer saw a middle-aged woman. A confident athlete with a glimmer of defiance stared back at me. For a split second I didn't recognize her.

Then I stood up straight, toothpaste foam on my face and said, "Yes Marybeth, you're an athlete again."

Many nights I woke up at 3 A.M. and my bravado gave way to fear—of trucks running us down, injuries, arguments and the enormity of the project. Was I up to this? Would I be able to get in shape? I was in my mid-fifties after all and hadn't competed in an athletic event for twenty-five years. After my girls were born I let go of the athlete within me.

For several weeks I didn't tell anyone and wrestled with the idea in my mind. Finally I shared my thoughts with my husband and he asked, "Are you sure?"

In the time leading up to our venture I formulated a plan and followed workouts with my trainer. Slowly I built up my endurance and confidence. I started with slow rides on flat terrain, but now I can pedal fifty-plus miles a day, day-after- day. My daughters believed I could do it and so did the super guy I married. He was behind us 100 percent.

And I have a new identity. Now I look in the mirror and say, "Hot damn, you're an athlete." It feels good to work out and it felt great to move toward fulfilling my goal.

Some vignettes stuck with me coast to coast, and I've included some of these in the following excerpts from our blog.

Meeting a Mountain Man in Utah

I was banging on the washer trying to make it work when the owner of the campground offered to help me. We'd stopped for the night in a small town in Utah. Duane had long grey hair and a bushy beard and smelled like mountain dirt and sweat. He was curious about us and I was curious about him. He listened as I briefly explained our bike trip. Like everyone we met, he was surprised to meet a mother daughter team.

While I folded clothes he told me about his life, the hardships of small town living, the long, cold winters, the short summers, and his love for fishing. He explained that for years he hunted deer and elk to feed his family.

Around dusk he tapped on the door of our camper with gifts of fresh rainbow trout caught that afternoon and a shoulder of frozen elk he had shot and dressed the previous fall. The next night we followed his instructions and marinated the elk in Italian salad dressing and grilled it over hot coals. Another evening we sautéed the trout in butter. We were touched by his generosity.

In the corn fields of Kansas

I stopped for a cold drink at a dusty, two-pump gas station at the intersection of two country roads in southeast Kansas. JC rode ahead. It was a sweltering Sunday morning too early for church goers but not too early for an old timer to sit on a bench in the shade with his morning coffee, cigarettes and bacon-flavored Cheez-Its.

"Good morning and why are you out so early today?" asked the elderly man in denim overalls. I lingered for a moment and looked into his eyes. They were droopy, kind eyes, and I made the kind of decision that can turn a day upside down—the decision to stop, sit on the bench and let time slow down.

Ed was born twenty miles up the road in a small town and now lives three miles down the road in a smaller one. He'd spent his life painting houses in rural southeast Kansas. His battered pick-up truck was parked next to the sleepy Licking Lizard Café behind the gas station.

Conversation flowed easily although there were moments when we didn't say anything at all. We just sat, watched the corn fields and listened to the birds.

When the occasional pick-up truck pulled up to the gas pump Ed always knew who it was and exchanged a few words with them. Each person left chuckling. Then he'd tell me a little something about each person as they drove away. "Now that guy works from sun-up to sun-down fixing oil rigs in the fields. Honest man." Or, "He's a fireman and today's his day off but he's helping to build the mud pit for the mud races on the Fourth of July." Ed wasn't a gossip and he had a kind word to say about everyone.

Between the silences we rambled from subject to subject touching on everything from legalizing marijuana to choosing the freshest corn on the cob. We discussed trusting people he told me about the nation's largest oil well which just so happened to be down the road and we had missed it. Ed didn't talk about his private life or his ailments. He pondered the past and the present. The future didn't exist.

Ed asked where I came from. "I didn't care much for California when I went to visit cousins in the Central Valley. I never went back. The stores were too big and everyone was in a hurry," he explained. "Here, everyone knows everyone. Yep, families have been here for generations." He was silent for a moment and added, "Small towns around here are biblical in some ways. They haven't changed much."

Sitting and taking with Ed made me happy because he has a gift—he finds the best in everyone.

Back onto the narrow, shoulder-less road with hazy corn fields and Ed at my back, I was headed for the Missouri border. It's amazing how a comfortable conversation with a stranger can renew a person.

A Lesson from Strangers

We stopped biking early one day to go to a Farmer's Market in Eureka, Kansas (population 2,916) in an effort to find some fresh tomatoes. We didn't find any tomatoes but what we did find was even better.

Vendors were packing up their pick-ups when we arrived and the tomatoes were long gone. Two picnic tables were still covered with home-canned sweet pickles, corn relish, butter squash, apple butter, pear butter and a variety of jellies.

JC headed straight for the cutest little guy in the state—a chatty, blonde two year old playing with a shiny green John Deere toy tractor. JC has a way with kids and entered his world easily. I heard him tell her, "My name is Sutton. I am two and my daddy's a cowboy." Sutton's mom, a slender, attractive young woman shook her head and laughed, then showed us her garden-fresh veggies and home-canned goods. We bought hot-tomato jelly, zucchini, cucumber and squash.

Stephanie had a confident yet easy and approachable manner. We talked about chigger bites and remedies, skipping from topic to topic the way women do when multi-tasking—and Stephanie is a master multi-tasker. She's the mother of two toddlers, married to an active cowboy and manages a huge garden with five dogs, cats, chickens and, oh yes, horses.

I asked Stephanie if anything was going on in town that evening, which led us to a conversation about how things used to be. "Our town is dying. In the past we had oil, but now it's just cows, horses and pastures. The Saturday night horse races were discontinued due to lack of government money, but we do have a "show-dee-o" tonight and you're welcome to come," she offered. She described it as a local "let the kids show off with their horses" rodeo where no one gets bucked off a horse and anyone can participate. Participation costs $1 per event and there's no minimum age limit so Karinne, her three-year-old daughter, would ride their "child broken" horse.

Stephanie gave us directions to the unmarked site where the Saddle Club of Greenwood County hosts the monthly "Show-dee-o." "Please join us and meet my husband, my daughter and my parents. We'll save you a space in the shade and I'll bring you some fresh eggs".

There are usually about 120 participants, but in June the crowd was thin because many families were harvesting, haying or planting. We had a great night of family fun at the Kiddie Rodeo with Stephanie and three generations of Kansas ranchers, businessmen and cowboys. Her parents welcomed us like kin, her husband explained horses and rodeo events and they all introduced us to friends. We cheered for Karrine when she took second place in the horse showmanship competition. She also completed in a contest to take a ribbon off the tail of a goat. Then she lassoed a plastic calf-head mounted on a bale of hay.

We listened to stories about frigid winters spent trapping and hunting coyotes, turkey, bobcats and deer. The men asked if we'd ever eaten "Mountain Oysters" and then told us about a nearby town's Wild Testicle Festival where "a bull stops here and leaves a steer."

As we pedaled out of town early the next morning we wondered why the people we met in Kansas were so easy to approach, so easy to talk to and so genuine. I think they're just comfortable with themselves, like Stephanie. JC and I vowed to be more hospitable to visitors when we got home.

The experience proved to be a valuable lesson for me and JC as we discussed our desire to be more spontaneous and hospitable to strangers like our Kansas friends had so been.

Reconnecting with Family in the Midwest

Dinners in the screened-in porch on the lake are a family tradition.

Every summer, four generations of my family ranging from our ninety-year-old grandma to new babies gather to fire up the grill and reconnect.

We took a detour from the bike route to visit with my family in Ohio.

Kids ran in and out and underneath us in the crowded house on Lake Erie. After the older kids trickled in from the beach they set the picnic table with the red-checkered tablecloth. In the kitchen we women shucked the corn, peeled fresh peaches and made iced tea. The men, including my husband who had flown in for the weekend, grilled burgers and told whopping fishing stories.

When the burgers were ready and everyone rounded up, we all sat down at the long table and said Grace and I felt like I'd slipped into a Norman Rockwell painting.

For over two decades we have descended upon my sister and her family at their summer home to eat too much, talk late into the night and watch the kids catch fire flies in the yard.

Shadows of sadness seeped into the dark corners of the porch. We spoke of family members who were not with us—my dad who has passed away, grown children in Africa, siblings far away, and our mom, who can no longer travel. In past years the table was longer and more crowded.

We visited my mom at her retirement home in Akron. When we drove up in our RV, she and her friends were rocking in wicker chairs by the front door waiting for us. When we descended from the RV, they applauded and cheered! Ah, no matter how old you are, it feels great when your mom is proud of you.

Like every family we have problems, tragedies, deaths and conflict amongst ourselves, but for two days we relaxed and just enjoyed being together again.

Kentucky

This morning at 6 A.M. when we opened the door of the R.V., it was there. In the grass, on the trees and over the hills. Humidity. Steamy, dripping, fog-up-your-glasses humidity.

JC and I try to follow my mom's advice: if you can't say something positive, don't say anything at all. We were cranky and quiet most of the day. If one of us starts complaining it's all downhill. Truth be told, it's hard to be stoic and tough day after day. It was tough getting up day-after-day to ride another sixty to eighty miles.

Today we rode in a 90-degree sauna through green pastures and bright-leafed tobacco fields dotted with small farms and grazing horses. We labored straight up steep hills then coasted down, down, precipitously into wooded gorges. Most of the roads of broken pavement and gravel were narrow with no shoulders.

The houses grew further and further apart and broken down automobiles and trucks cluttered their yards. Rusted-out washing machines, refrigerators and dilapidated sofas were crammed onto porches.

An old man in overalls rocking on the screened-in porch of his unpainted cabin stared at us as we passed. We noticed him watching us and waved. He raised his index finger an inch in acknowledgment and kept rocking. JC thought he had a menacing look. I didn't have the same vibe, but then I'm the older woman.

In Booneville I stopped to read a historical marker about Civil War activity in the area when a farmer selling corn from the back of his pick-up asked me, "How's this weather for ya?" I responded, "Hot, mighty hot." He asked, "How're those hills for ya?" I answered, "Tough, mighty tough." He nodded and warned me, "Gunna git worse." He was right.

As I pedaled out of Booneville I glanced up at the digital clock on the bank. It flashed the time and temperature; 11:05 A.M. and 90 degrees and 80% humidity.

We were warned by cross-country bikers we met riding toward us that Eastern Kentucky could be dangerous because of wild dogs and heavy coal truck traffic. The coal trucks drive fast, the roads are windy and they can't see you until they're on top of you. Sometimes the coal falls off the rigs. We were nervous.

Several times ferocious canines jumped out of the underbrush next to the road. Surprised by the dog's leap for my ankles and his growling, teeth-gnashing ferocity, I screamed bloody murder and pedaled for my life. JC, who was pedaling ahead up the hill, glanced back at me and I saw her terror. She has assumed a very protective attitude toward her mom and she had no control over this potential crisis. We are wearing dog whistles around our necks, but it takes a few seconds to get them into your mouth and blow. My instinct to push hard and escape worked.

The weather got hotter, the riding got tougher and we blogged less as we pushed on for the Atlantic Coast.

The Finale

On a blistering summer day when the temperature hit 108 degrees at 10 A.M., we slowly pedaled the last twelve miles on the Colonial Parkway from Williamsburg to Yorktown, Virginia; the official end of the TransAmerica Bike Route. We dipped our front tires into the Atlantic, snapped quick pictures and plunged into the cool water. I've rarely looked worse and felt so simultaneously triumphant and exhausted. We hobbled to a nearby air-conditioned restaurant featuring brunch with a "bottomless Mimosa" and lingered in a stupor for the rest of the sweltering afternoon.

Many feelings surfaced—relief, gratitude, and accomplishment. We made it. And we made it without major accidents. Yes there were bruises and blood, but no broken bones or fractured relationships.

During the five-hour flight home, across 3,000 miles, we looked down at the plains, the rivers and the deserts and mused about the summer we had spent slowly pedaling across this vast and beautiful land. As I closed my eyes for a much-needed nap, I thought, "I love this country. I love my family and I'm so glad this ride is over and I'm going home."

A mother-daughter rite of passage

The two months that JC and I spent together biking across the USA was not been a vacation; it was a rigorous physical challenge as well as a test of managing stress, maximizing patience and pulling together as partners.

Unlike many riders we met along the way, we weren't part of a big bike group that offers the added safety of experienced leaders, many riders and someone making your meals. After a full day of riding, we did our laundry, shopping, and cooking before we bunked down in the camper that followed us. The bike trip was hard work.

JC and I experienced a "rite of passage" in our relationship. We took care of each other on the road and in many other ways.

At times JC "mothered" me, bringing me ice packs, massaging my sore shoulder and insisting that I eat more and sleep longer. I depended on her to map our directions, fix the computer, download photos, and lift anything heavy. We calmed each other in the face of potential tornadoes, wild dog attacks, heat stroke and semitrucks blasting us off the road.

The mother-daughter hierarchy we knew at the beginning of the trip has been forever shattered. My role as mother has shifted from authority to partnership. We are equals and friends and share a very deep love and respect for each other. I like it that way. I doubt we will ever have two months together again. JC lives in another city and our lives diverged when the bike ride ended.

Although we rode 3,115 miles from California to Virginia, we feel our greatest achievement was to raise $52,000 for the National Osteoporosis Foundation. Our goal was to increase awareness of women's bone health. We had over 15,000 fans on Facebook who followed our progress and many contributed.

I'm proud to say we did it, but I would never do it again.

BEST PLACES TO HEAL

Find what works for you.

My mother shared her love of gardening with me when I was young, and when she died after a long illness, I planted myself in my garden to tear out weeds and wail to the winds.

Two months after her passing, I was on a business trip in Los Angeles and tacked on a few hours to make a pilgrimage in her honor to the glorious Huntington Botanical Garden in Pasadena. Because Mom instilled in me her passion for roses, I wandered through the 104-year-old rose garden. Closing my eyes, I felt her presence as I inhaled sweet fragrance of our favorite roses: Peace, Double Delight and Just Joey. Just being still among the roses with Mom was therapeutic in a way her funeral never could have been.

I'm not one to wallow in sadness for long. I learned long ago that the fastest way to drown my sorrows was to take a trip. Traveling helps me re-center, and it reminds me how much I can do, how much I can give, and how much beauty there is in the world.

So when my brother died after a long battle with cancer, I knew what I had to do. I grabbed my backpack and hiking boots and set off for the Grand Teton National Park in Wyoming.

Hiking has always been a direct, physical way for me to release my rage, sorrow and sense of helplessness. Nothing puts my life and mortality into sharper perspective than hiking in the grandeur of mountains and forests. The power and resilience of the towering trees and rigid rocks help me push my life's difficulties to the side and connect me to something bigger than myself.

It's not only life's tragedies that send me packing. Sometimes, when my spirit starts to flag a little, or I'm in a funk or (those "menopause moments"), I organize a short road trip with my closest girlfriends. Roll down the windows, crank up the tunes, sing or talk it out and let the miles of highway roll behind you.

Nothing compares with the companionship of close women friends—from my childhood, college or newer friends who are the mothers of grown children. When we travel together we have uninterrupted time to share our deepest feelings and to listen with compassionate attention. I need the adventure, the laughter and healing power of "girl talk." I'm fortunate to not only have a great husband, but one who encourages me to travel with my friends so I can "talk it over and talk it out" and return to him uplifted and revived.

I'm also lucky to live in the San Francisco Bay area, an easy launch pad for a five-to-seven day trip to Canyon Country in the southwest. I fly to Phoenix or Las Vegas, pick up a rental car and explore the National and State parks of Utah, Colorado, Arizona and New Mexico where I feel my deepest spiritual connection with the red rock canyons and moonlike landscapes under blindingly blue skies.

One of my favorite pick-me-up road trips is the Grand Circle Loop. Driving through the red rock pinnacles and buttes, thick Ponderosa forests and wide-open desert gives me a sense of liberation unlike anything else. Windows down, hair blowing, music blasting, I feel free, alert and alive. Depending on how much time I can steal, I might stop in Zion, Bryce or Grand Canyon national parks, or Arizona's Monument Valley or Colorado's Mesa Verde.

Although my chosen path to healing is to immerse myself in the raw beauty of nature, with its vast spaces and silences, sometimes—when I'm in need of some deep pampering—I sometimes head to a spa for my healing. Everyone has their own way of healing. For me it's taking a trip. I return home renewed and with a healthier perspective on my loss as well as the remaining time in my own life. So I'll keep traveling until my heart stops beating.

XXII

THE FINAL WORD

Through travel I first became aware of the outside world; it was
through travel that I found my own introspective way
into becoming a part of it.

—*Eudora Welty*

"HOW HAS TRAVEL CHANGED your life?" someone once asked
me in an interview. Travel has changed me in many ways. It's made
me more aware of the world around me. It's brought extraordinary people into my life. It's taught me to give up control. It's deepened my sense of empathy and concern for people worldwide. In
answering the question, though, it's made me deeply comfortable
with myself. Before I traveled around the world at age twenty-nine,
I had never gone to a movie or out to eat alone. Now, after years of
travel and risk taking, I savor the moments I have to myself. I have
learned to listen deeply to myself, and to have confidence in my
choices. I am a Gutsy Woman.

Gutsy does not mean fearless. On the contrary—it means coming
close enough to our fears that we realize the depth of our courage.

And through travel, we come to know and summon that courage. For as we leave our well-trod terrain and all that is familiar
behind, we leave our comfort zones. Whether communicating in
a new language, finding our way through a foreign city, or tasting
strange new food, travel challenges and stretches us. As we test ourselves, we break through limiting ideas of ourselves. We discover
that we are more than what we thought; we can do more than we
imagined. We can break with tradition, try on new roles, cross
boundaries imposed by society or the routines of our day-to-day

lives. As we travel, we reclaim our sense of self and strength. Travel takes us to the core of ourselves, and it changes us.

My hope, thus, is that the tips, wisdom, and personal anecdotes presented in this third edition of Gutsy Women will help inform and illuminate your own unique path—the one that draws you boldly out into the world and, inevitably, bravely into yourself. I hope that the voices of the many women quoted in this book have inspired you to crack open your own fears and discover the treasures within.

So be a Gutsy Woman—you know you already are! Take a trip—it doesn't matter if it's a monthlong trek in the Himalayas or a daylong excursion to a local beach. What's important is trying something new, something compelling, and maybe even a little scary. Something you've dreamed about. Whatever it is, try it. See how it feels. See what you learn about yourself. It may be something you never imagined. Something wonderful. Something surprising. Something . . . gutsy.

XXIII
RESOURCES

―――

WOMEN TOUR SERVICES

AdventureWomen
www.adventurewomen.com

The Women's Travel Club
www.womenstravelclub.com

Canyon Calling Tours
www.canyoncalling.com

Mariah Wilderness Expeditions
www.mariahwe.com

Northwest Women's Surf Camps & Retreats
www.nwwomenssurfcamps.com

Adventures in Good Company
www.adventuresingoodcompany.com

Women Tours (Bike Trips)
www.womantours.com

Sheri Griffith Expeditions
www.griffithexp.com

Call of the Wild
www.callwild.com

Gutsy Women Travel
www.gutsywomentravel.com

Canadian Woman Traveler
www.cwtraveller.ca

Adventure Associates
www.adventureassociates.net

Women Traveling Together
www.women-traveling.com

Adventurous Wench
www.adventurouswench.com

Chicks Climbing
www.chickswithpicks.net

Mind Over Mountains
www.mindovermountains.com

Babes in the Backcountry
www.Babesinthebackcountry.com

Women-Traveling
http://www.women-traveling.com

Wanderlust and Lipstick
http://wanderlustandlipstick.com

Serendipity Traveler
http://www.serendipitytraveler.com

Adventurous Wench.
http://www.adventurouswench.com/

BOOMER TRAVEL

Road Scholar (Formerly Elderhostel)

Grand Circle *Travel* www.gct.com

Grand European Tours http://www.getours.com/
http://www.babyboomertrips.com/
Silversea Senior Cruises www.Silversea.com

Senior Tours Canada *www.seniortours.ca*
Accessible and Disability Travel
www.disabledtravelers.com/travel_agents.htm
Suddenly Senior
www.suddenlysenior.com

AARP www.aarp.org

Singles Travel Company
www.singlestravelcompany.com

VOLUNTEER TRAVEL

Volunteer Projects Abroad | i-to-i.com
www.i-to-i.com/Volunteer_Projects

International Volunteer - Most Affordable Volunteer Org.
www.volunteerhq.org/Abroad

Different Travel - Home
www.different-travel.com

Nomad Adventure Travel Store
www.nomadtravel.co.uk

Cross Cultural Solutions
www.crossculturalsolutions.org
Like a Mini Peace Corps

Volunteer Travel | VOA.org
www.voa.org

OneWorld365 : Meaningful Travel, Volunteer Projects,
Adventure . . .
www.oneworld365.org

Volunteer Travel Abroad | volunteeralliance.org
www.volunteeralliance.org/Travel

Habitat for Humanity - International Volunteer Programs
www.habitat.org/Volunteers

Responsible Travel
www.responsibletravel.com/holidays/volunteer-travel
EarthWatch www.earthwatch.org

Travel Nursing Volunteers - Travel Nursing Central
www.travelnursingcentral.com/volunteer.html

Women Travel The World Volunteer Networks
http://www.womentravel.info

HOMESTAYS

www.homestayfinder.com
Greenheart *Travel Homestay* Abroad Programs

www.cci-exchange.com/homestaysabroad.aspx
CouchSurfing –www.couchsurfing.org
Hospitality Club. An online hospitality exchange organization
http://www.hospitalityclub.org/

Rent a room in a locals home
www.airbnb.com
http://www.womentravel.info/

Packing List

CLOTHING

___ belts
___ blouse
___ boots
___ coats
___ dresses
___ gloves
___ hats
___ jackets
___ jeans

___ long t-shirts
___ panties
___ pantyhose
___ rain/sun hat
___ raincoat
___ scarves
___ shirts
___ shoes, dress
___ shoes, walking

___ shorts
___ slacks
___ slippers
___ socks
___ suits
___ sweat suit
___ sweaters
___ swimsuits
___ body cream

HYGIENE

___ brush/comb
___ dental floss
___ deodorant
___ face soap
___ foot powder
___ Kleenex
___ lip balm
___ magnifying mirror
___ moleskin

___ makeup
___ nail brush
___ nail clippers
___ nail file
___ nail polish remover
___ razor/blades
___ shampoo/ conditioner
___ sunblock

___ surgical face mask
___ or kerchief
___ tampons
___ toothpaste
___ tweezers
___ antihistamines
___ antibiotic ointment

MEDICAL

___ antiseptic skin cleanser

___ Band-aids

___ birth control

___ contact lenses and supplies

___ cotton swabs

___ diarrhea medicine

___ insect repellant

___ motion sickness remedy

___ muscle relaxant

___ nasal spray

___ Pepto Bismol / Alka Seltzer

___ prescription glasses (extra pair and copy of prescription)

___ prescription medications

___ sleeping pills

___ Sting Stop (insert Trade mark sign) gels

___ thermometer

___ address book

___ credit cards

DOCUMENTS

___ driver's license

___ family pictures (in plastic cover)

___ maps

___ passport / visas

___ passport photos (include extras)

___ photocopies of passport / visas

___ student ID card

___ travel insurance

___ travel tickets

MISCELLANEOUS

___ alarm clock

___ batteries

___ calculator

___ camera / film

___ cash

___ clothesline

___ corkscrew

___ earplugs

___ electrical converter & adapter plugs

___ eyeshades

___ filmshield

___ flashlight

___ games / playing cards

___ guidebooks

___ highlighter pen (to mark maps)

___ journal

___ laundry detergent / Woolite

___ luggage locks (combination)

___ luggage tags

___ pens / pencils

___ phrase book

___ pillowcase (doubles as laundry bag)

___ pocket calculator

___ reading material

___ rubber bands

MISCELLANEOUS
(*CONTINUED*)

___ rubber door
stopper
___ safety pins
___ scissors
___ sewing kit

___ stationery
___ sunglasses
___ digital tape
recorder
___ watch

___ water bottle
___ whistle
___ zip-lock bags

ACKNOWLEDGMENTS

I HAVE BEEN TOLERATED and my absences in mind and body forgiven by my patient, loving husband Gary and my heart's great joy: my daughters.

Three decades of my own travel experiences and a broad wealth of other travelers' wisdom have gone into the making of Gutsy Women. I couldn't have completed this book without help.

My heartfelt thanks to those who helped me: James O'Reilly, Larry Habegger, and Natalie Baszile

Simply, sincerely, thank you to all of my travel buddies, writer colleagues, supportive friends, mentors, and role models who have inspired, advised, and encouraged me.

About the Author

LAST YEAR MARYBETH VISITED her 90th country. She has hiked, biked, dived, danced, snow-shoed, skied, climbed, coptered, trekked and traipsed her way through seven continents, from the depth of the Flores Sea to the summit of Mount Kilimanjaro. She has truly earned her reputation as "the trusted and experienced voice of travel." Along the way Mary.At twenty-nine, she took off again, this time to travel alone around the world. These two years of travel changed her life. She met her future husband, am American, in Kathmandu, Nepal, and she returned to begin a new career as a writer, online travel magazine publisher, spokesperson, and speaker. Since then she has spoken around the world at such venues as the Explorer's Club and Asia Society in New York and at conventions and corporate meetings.

Marybeth's first book, *A Woman's World,* is a best-seller and won the Lowell Thomas Gold Medal for the Best Travel Book from the Society of American Travel Writers Foundation.

Marybeth was a featured guest on the Oprah Winfrey Show, with her book *Gutsy Women*. As a nationally recognized travel expert and media personality, Marybeth has appeared on CBS News, CNN, ABC, NBC, and National Public Radio. She was the "Smart Traveler" radio host for the nationally syndicated Outside Radio show and the travel expert/columnist for the Travel Channel on ivillage.com.

She is currently the Publisher of the online travel magazine GutsyTraveler.com, Adventure Correspondent for *TravelGirl Magazine*, Special Travel Contributor to CNN Television and "Official Sightseer" spokesperson for Transitions Lenses.

Marybeth has two daughters, a husband, and a rescue dog and lives in Northern California. She travels as much as she can—with her family, girlfriends, or alone. Is she still gutsy? Two years ago she and her daughter biked 3,115 miles across the USA from the Pacific to the Atlantic Ocean, for a challenge, adventure and her favorite charity. They raised $52,000 for the National Osteoporosis Foundation through their blog and sponsors.

Follow along with her on the travel magazine www.Gutsy Traveler.com.